Microwave Cooking · On a Diet

Litton Microwave Cooking Products, Minneapolis, Minnesota

CERTIFIED FOR
MICROWAVE COOKING

LITTON
Microwave
Cooking
Center

CREDITS:
Design & Production: Cy DeCosse Creative Department, Inc.
Author: Barbara Methven
Dietitians: Karen Rubin, Jeanne Moe
Home Economists: Jill Crum, Peggy Lamb, Susan Pence, Nancy Johnson, Carol Grones, Susan Failor, Grace Wells, Sylvia Ogren, Barbara Strand
Food Stylists: Akiko Yamamoto, Maria Rolandelli, Susan Finley
Photographers: Michael Jensen, Steven Smith, Ken Greer
Production Coordinators: Mary Ann Knox, Delores Swanson, Christine Watkins
Consumer Testers: Judith Richard, Sue Lowenberg, Robyn Cook, Patty Waite, Gail Bailey, Diana Jones, Anne Antolak
Color Separations: Weston Engraving Co., Inc.
Printing: Moebius Printing Co.

This is no ordinary recipe book. It's like a cooking school in your home, ready to answer questions on the spot. Step-by-step photographs show you how to prepare food for microwaving, what to do during cooking, how to tell when the food is done. A new photo technique shows you how foods look during microwaving.

The foods selected for this book are basic in several ways. All microwave well and demonstrate the advantages of microwaving. They are popular foods you prepare frequently, so the book will be useful in day-to-day cooking. Each food illustrates a principle or technique of microwaving which you can apply to similar recipes you find in magazines or other cookbooks.

This book was designed to obtain good results in all brands of ovens. Techniques may vary from the cookbook developed for your oven. If rotating foods is unnecessary in your oven, that technique may be eliminated. All foods are cooked at either High or 50% power (Medium). The Defrost setting on earlier ovens and Simmer setting on current ovens may be used when Medium is called for. This simplifies the choice of settings while you become familiar with the reasons why different foods require different power levels.

Microwaving is easy as well as fast. The skills you develop with this book will help you make full and confident use of your microwave oven.

The Litton Microwave
Cooking Center

Contents

THE LOW SODIUM COOK BOOK — Payne & Callahan — Little, Brown

Craig Claiborne's Gourmet Diet

Living With High Blood Pressure

WEIGHT WATCHERS' NEW PROGRAM COOKBOOK

The American Heart Association — DAVID McKAY

The GOURMET LOW-CALORIE Kitchen — HELEN BELINKIE

What You Need to Know Before You Start

This is a cookbook, not a diet book. It doesn't dictate what you can or should eat. It is designed to show you how the microwave oven can make the foods on your diet flavorful, nutritious, attractive and easy to prepare. If you're simply interested in eating a little lighter, you'll find a lot of your favorite recipes, reformulated along less fattening lines. Each recipe gives you the per serving calculations for calories, sodium, cholesterol and exchanges, so you can fit them into your own dieting plan. If you have special dietary needs, your diet should be approved by a dietitian or your doctor. But a diet that allows for your food preferences will be the most effective one. From this book, you can select foods that not only fit your diet but taste good, too.

A Microwave Oven is the Dieter's Best Friend

Many diets call for cooking procedures which, when done conventionally, are time-consuming and difficult to achieve. These procedures are inherent in microwaving and the results are delicious.

Microwaving Requires Little Fat

While some fat is necessary in your diet, many diets restrict the amount or type of fat consumed. Fat is not required to microwave food, so the fat allowance in your diet can be used for eye and appetite appeal, instead.

Microwaving Makes Sensible Eating Easier

With microwaving, you'll find you can prepare light, nutritious meals quickly. If you have to wait an hour for dinner to cook conventionally, you may be more likely to snack on fattening foods. In the time it would take to fix some cheese and crackers, you could microwave a piece of chicken or fish. Your diet can be tailored to individual needs because single servings are so easy to prepare. Leftovers are also ideally suited to microwaving because food doesn't dry out or lose flavor when reheated.

Lean foods, like fish fillets or skinned chicken can be easily microwaved without using fat, special pans or additives to prevent sticking.

Microwaving Retains Nutrients

Many vitamins and minerals are water soluble or heat-sensitive. They are dissolved and drained away in cooking water or are destroyed by prolonged cooking. Little or no water is needed to microwave vegetables, so vitamins and minerals are not lost with drained cooking liquid.

Microwaving Brings Out Flavor

In diets which call for salt-free and fat-free cooking, the natural good taste of foods is significant. Microwaving intensifies flavors. A little seasoning goes a long way. Salt is added after cooking and can even be eliminated in most cases, if desired.

Microwaving Enhances Appetite Appeal

When you're dieting, the texture and appearance of food is doubly important. Microwaving cooks food tender while retaining its color, shape and texture.

Compare the appearance, flavor and nutrition of microwaved broccoli with conventionally cooked. Green liquid from conventional cooking contains nutrients and flavors which will be discarded before serving.

How To Use This Book

The recipes in this book provide good tasting dishes with low calorie content. The nutritional information following every recipe lists the per serving measurement of calories, sodium, cholesterol and exchanges. This measurement includes ingredients listed as optional. Use this information to select recipes which fit your personal diet.

Serving Sizes

Portion control is important in any diet. These recipes should provide satisfying amounts of food. Every recipe lists a serving size.

Special Diets

The nutritional information following each recipe helps you use the book with several popular diets. Follow the recommendations of your physician or dietitian for the amount and types of food you should eat.

Calories. For the benefit of calorie counters and dieters using an exchange system, the per serving calorie level is given with each recipe. In some cases, minimal amounts of high calorie foods, such as margarine, have been included for flavor. Artificial sweeteners have not been used because they do not give uniform results.

Low Sodium. The per serving sodium level for each recipe is measured using the ingredients listed. To reduce sodium further, omit salt and use a salt substitute, light soy sauce, or low-salt bouillon and catsup. Where sodium levels are high, suggestions are given for substituting other ingredients.

Low Cholesterol. The per serving cholesterol measurement is based on the ingredients listed, using polyunsaturated margarine and oils. Where cholesterol levels are high, due to the presence of saturated fats, substitute ingredients are suggested.

Exchange System. This method of dieting is recommended by physicians, dietitians, and weight control groups because it provides a varied menu, sound nutrition, easy-to-use portion control, and simplified calorie counting. Exchanges are listed with each recipe and in the tables provided on pages 8 to 13.

Meatballs With Tomato & Green Pepper Sauce ▲

Tomato & Green Pepper
Sauce, page 129
1 lb. extra lean ground beef
1 egg
½ cup grated carrot
½ teaspoon salt, optional
¼ teaspoon pepper

Serves 4

Prepare Tomato & Green Pepper Sauce as directed. Set aside. Blend remaining ingredients. Form into 12 meatballs. Arrange in 12 × 8-in. baking dish. Cover with wax paper. Microwave at High 6 to 9 minutes, or until meatballs are firm and no longer pink, rearranging after half the cooking time. Drain; set aside.

Microwave sauce at High 1 to 3 minutes, or until heated through. Serve over meatballs.

Per Serving:
Calories: 237
Sodium: 590 mg.
Cholesterol: 140 mg.
Exchanges: 2 vegetable, 3 low fat meat, ½ fat

52

Taco Dinner Salad

1 lb. extra lean ground be
1 medium onion, choppe
¼ cup catsup
2 teaspoons chili powde
1 teaspoon ground cum
½ teaspoon salt, optiona
¼ teaspoon pepper
6 cups shredded lettuc
2 large tomatoes, chop

In 1-qt. casserole comb
crumbled ground beef
onion. Microwave at H
minutes, or until beef i
longer pink, stirring or
twice. Drain well. Stir
chili powder, cumin, :
pepper. Microwave a
to 3½ minutes, or ur
stirring once or twic

Divide lettuce and t
4 serving bowls. Ac
ground beef mixtur
bowl; toss if desire

NOTE: for low sod
substitute low-salt

Per Serving:
Calories: 19
Sodium: 50
Cholesterol: 77
Exchanges: 1'
                3

Microwave Gives Leaner, Lighter Foods

Many people, even though they're not following a diet, are interested in trimming calorie, cholesterol and sodium consumption to improve their health and personal appearance.

The recipes in this book are designed to give you food that is appetizing and flavorful while reducing calories, sodium and cholesterol levels.

Compare these recipes. Where conventional cooking calls for 6 tablespoons of fat to brown chicken and prevent sticking, the standard microwave recipe trims calories to 304 per serving by reducing butter. And the diet version reduces calories even further, to 221, by eliminating the butter and substituting whole milk yogurt for the dairy sour cream.

Conventional Paprika Chicken

4 tablespoons butter	1 tablespoon paprika
2 tablespoons salad oil	½ cup finely chopped onion
2½ to 3½ lb. broiler-fryer chicken, cut up	¼ cup dry white wine
Salt and pepper	1 cup dairy sour cream

Serves 4

Melt butter in skillet with oil. Add chicken pieces; brown. Sprinkle with seasonings. Add onions and wine. Reduce heat; cover. Cook 25 to 30 minutes, or until tender. Remove chicken. Blend in cream; heat and pour over chicken.

Per Serving:
Calories: 543   Cholesterol: 199 mg.
Sodium: 434 mg.   Exchanges: 3 med. fat meat, 6½ fat

Microwave Paprika Chicken

2 tablespoons butter	1 tablespoon paprika
2½ to 3½ lb. broiler-fryer chicken, cut up	½ cup finely chopped onion
	2 tablespoons dry white wine
Salt and pepper	1 cup dairy sour cream

Serves 4

In casserole melt butter at High 45 to 60 seconds. Add chicken; turn to coat. Sprinkle with seasonings. Add onion and wine; cover. Microwave at High 15 to 18 minutes, or until juices run clear; turn and rearrange after half the time. Remove chicken. Skim fat. Blend in cream. Reduce power to 50% (Medium). Microwave 1½ to 2½ minutes to heat. Pour over chicken.

Per Serving:
Calories: 304   Cholesterol: 64 mg.
Sodium: 405 mg.   Exchanges: 3 med. fat meat, 3½ fat

Diet Microwave Paprika Chicken

2½ to 3½ lb. broiler-fryer chicken, cut up, skin removed	1 tablespoon paprika
	½ cup finely chopped onion
	2 tablespoons dry white wine
Dash salt, optional	1 cup whole milk yogurt
Dash pepper	

Serves 4

Arrange chicken in casserole. Sprinkle with seasonings. Add onion and wine; cover. Microwave at High 15 to 18 minutes, or until juices run clear; turn and rearrange after half the time. Remove chicken. Skim fat. Blend in yogurt. Reduce power to 50% (Medium). Microwave 1½ to 2½ minutes. Pour over chicken.

Per Serving:
Calories: 221   Cholesterol: 39 mg.
Sodium: 305 mg.   Exchanges: 3 low fat meat, ½ fat

A Word About Nutrition

Nutrients are the elements in food which the body uses to build and maintain itself. The essential nutrients—water, protein, carbohydrates, minerals, vitamins and fat—are necessary for survival.

Why Fad Diets Don't Work. Any diet which eliminates an essential nutrient or over-emphasizes one type of food at the expense of others can lead to health problems. Even if you take vitamin and mineral supplements, a fad diet may result in nutritional deficiencies. There may be an initial weight loss; frequently, what is lost is body fluid rather than stored fat. One-food diets are boring, even if you like the food. Weight which is lost quickly is also regained quickly. A good reducing diet maintains health, promotes good eating patterns, and produces steady and reasonable weight loss.

How the Body Uses Food. Nutrients often work in combination. If one is deficient or lacking, the body cannot

Seven Major Food Groups

Meat, poultry, seafood, eggs, and cheese provide complete protein, which builds tissue and fights infection. They also contribute vitamins, minerals and fat. If you are on a low calorie or low cholesterol diet, keep in mind that even though these foods are all high protein, some contain more fat than others do.

Bread, cereals, rice, pasta and starchy vegetables provide high amounts of minerals and vita-mins, some protein and bulk to satisfy hunger.

Fats are high in calories and should be used sparingly and measured accurately. They do contain some vitamins and are an essential ingredient for good nutrition. Fat used in cooking or contained in foods like meat and whole milk add to your fat consumption. If you are on a low cholesterol diet, avoid saturated (animal) fats.

utilize the other. For example, if your body is to use protein to build tissue and fight infection, you must consume some carbohydrates for energy. A little fat is necessary to utilize certain vitamins. Proper balance of nutrients is essential. Since the body uses only what it needs, too much of some nutrients can be as harmful as a deficiency. Extra protein, carbohydrates and fats are stored in the body as fat, while excessive amounts of some vitamins can be dangerous. A balanced diet is one in which the food you eat provides all the essential nutrients in the proper balance without supplements.

Seven Food Groups Make a Good Diet. For proper nutrition, you should eat balanced amounts of these seven major food groups: meat, bread, fruits, vegetables, fats, milk, and the free foods. Your body will get the nutrients it needs while you enjoy a varied diet.

Fruits supply vitamins, minerals, carbohydrate sugar for energy and fiber which provides bulk in the diet.

Vegetables are a rich source of minerals, vitamins, fiber to aid digestion, and carbohydrates. They are generally low in calories, as well as in sodium and cholesterol content.

Milk is an important source of complete protein, carbohydrate, vitamins and minerals, especially calcium. An 8 oz. glass of fortified skim milk contains all the nutrients of whole milk without the saturated fat.

Free Foods contain little or no calories and can be used as seasoning, condiments, garnishes, beverages or as snacks.

How to Use the Exchange Charts

The exchange system has become a popular and useful tool for dieters in planning their daily food consumption. It combines calorie counting and basic food groups to make weight loss and good nutrition easier to manage.

Foods are divided into six groups, or Exchanges. They are grouped by comparable calorie and nutrient values—such as meats in one group, fruits in another. Foods in any one group can be exchanged with any other food in the same group. For example, 1 fruit exchange = 40 calories = 1 small apple = 2 medium plums. You should not make substitutions between groups, or increase one exchange at the expense of another. It takes all six groups working together to supply all the nutrients needed for a balanced diet.

Your diet will contain a given number of exchanges from the six groups to total the desired number of calories needed per day to maintain or lose weight. Instead of counting 1000 calories, you count 15 or 18 exchanges. Your diet will be evenly distributed between groups so you are assured of good nutrition. You make your own choices from each group. The exchange values of the recipes in this book have been calculated so you will know how they fit into your diet.

Fruit Exchanges: One Fruit Exchange contains 40 calories and 10 grams of carbohydrate.

Fruits are valuable for vitamins, minerals and fiber. Vitamin C is abundant in citrus fruits and fruit juices, and is contained in raspberries, strawberries, mangoes, cantaloupes, honeydews and papayas. The best sources of vitamin A among these fruits include fresh or dried apricots, mangoes, cantaloupes, nectarines, yellow peaches and persimmons. Many fruits are a valuable source of potassium, especially apricots, bananas, several of the berries, grapefruit, grapefruit juice, mangoes, cantaloupes, honeydews, nectarines, oranges, orange juice and peaches. Fruit may be used fresh, dried, canned or frozen, cooked or raw, as long as no sugar is added. This list shows the kinds and amounts of fruit to use for one Fruit Exchange.

Apple	1 small	Lemon juice	½ cup
Apple juice	⅓ cup	Lime juice	½ cup
Applesauce (unsweetened)	½ cup	Loquats	3
Apricots, fresh	2 medium	Lichee	6
Apricots, dried	4 halves	Mango	½ small
Banana	½ small	Nectarine	1 small
Blackberries	½ cup	Orange	1 small
Blueberries	½ cup	Orange juice	½ cup
Cantaloupe	¼ small	Papaya	¾ cup
Cherries	10 large	Passion fruit	1
Cranberries	Unlimited	Passion fruit juice	⅓ cup
Cranberry juice (sweetened)	¼ cup	Peach	1 medium
Cranberry juice (low calorie)	¾ cup	Peach nectar (sweetened)	⅓ cup
Cranberry juice (unsweetened)	Unlimited	Pear	1 small
Crenshaw melon	2-in. wedge	Pear nectar (unsweetened)	⅓ cup
Currants	2 tablespoons	Persimmon, native	1 medium
Dates	2	Pineapple	½ cup
Figs, fresh	1	Pineapple juice	⅓ cup
Figs, dried	1	Plantain	½ small
Fructose	1 tablespoon	Plums	2 medium
Grapefruit	½	Pomegranate	1 small
Grapefruit juice	½ cup	Prunes	2 small
Grapes	12	Prune juice	¼ cup
Grape juice	¼ cup	Raisins	2 tablespoons
Guava	⅔	Raspberries	½ cup
Honeydew melon	⅛ medium	Strawberries	¾ cup
Kiwi	1	Tangerine	1 medium
Kumquats, fresh	2	Watermelon	1 cup

Milk Exchanges: One Milk Exchange contains 80 calories, 12 grams of carbohydrate, 8 grams of protein and a trace of fat.

Milk is the leading source of calcium. It is a good source of phosphorous, protein, some of the B-complex vitamins, including folacin and vitamin B₁₂, and vitamins A and D. Magnesium is also found in milk. This list shows the amount of milk or milk products to use for one Milk Exchange.

Non-Fat Fortified Milk
Skim or non-fat milk . . . . 1 cup
Powdered (non-fat dry, before adding liquid) . . . . ⅓ cup
Canned, evaporated - skim milk . . . . ½ cup
Buttermilk made from skim milk . . . . 1 cup
Yogurt made from skim milk (plain, unflavored) . . . . 1 cup

The following milk products have ½ additional Fat Exchange and contain 100 calories.

Low-Fat Fortified Milk
1% fat fortified milk . . . . 1 cup
Canned, evaporated - low-fat milk . . . . ½ cup

The following milk products have 1 additional Fat Exchange and contain 125 calories.

2% fat fortified milk . . . . 1 cup
Yogurt made from 2% fortified milk (plain, unflavored) . . . . 1 cup

The following milk products have 2 additional Fat Exchanges and contain 170 calories.

Whole milk . . . . 1 cup
Canned, evaporated whole milk . . . . ½ cup
Buttermilk made from whole milk . . . . 1 cup
Yogurt made from whole milk (plain, unflavored) . . . . 1 cup

Vegetable Exchanges: One Vegetable Exchange contains 25 calories, about 5 grams of carbohydrate and 2 grams of protein.

Dark green and deep yellow vegetables are among the leading sources of vitamin A. Many of the vegetables in this group are good sources of vitamin C — asparagus, broccoli, Brussels sprouts, cabbage, cauliflower, collards, kale, spinach, rutabagas, tomatoes, turnips and dandelion, mustard and turnip greens. A number are particularly good sources of potassium — broccoli, Brussels sprouts, beet greens, chard, tomato juice. This list shows the kinds of vegetables to use for one Vegetable Exchange. One Exchange is ½ cup unless noted otherwise. Starchy vegetables are found in the Bread Exchanges list.

Alfalfa sprouts*	Chicory	Lettuce*	Spinach*
Artichoke	Chinese cabbage	Mushrooms*	Summer squash
Asparagus	Cilantro*	Mustard greens*	Tomatoes
Bamboo shoots	(coriander leaf)	Okra	Tomato juice
Bean sprouts	Chives*	Onions	Tomato paste
Beets	Collards	Palm heart	(2 tablespoons)
Beet greens	Cucumbers	Parsley*	Tomato puree
Broccoli	Dandelion*	Poke	(3 tablespoons)
Brussels sprouts	Eggplant	Radishes*	Tomato sauce (¼ cup)
Cabbage	Endive*	Red pepper	Turnips
Carrots	Escarole*	Rhubarb	Turnip greens
Cauliflower	Green beans	Romaine lettuce*	Vegetable juice cocktail
Celery	Green onions	Rutabaga	Water chestnuts (5)
Celery cabbage*	Green pepper	Sauerkraut	Watercress*
Celery root	Jerusalem artichokes	Soybeans	Wax beans
Chard*	Kale	Spaghetti squash	Zucchini
Chayote	Leeks		

*"free foods" — vegetables which contain negligible calories when eaten *raw*.

Bread Exchanges: (includes Breads, Cereals and Starchy Vegetables): One Bread Exchange contains 70 calories, 15 grams of carbohydrate and 2 grams of protein.

Whole grain and enriched breads and cereals, wheat germ and bran products, and dried beans and peas are good sources of iron and thiamin. Wheat germ, bran, dried beans, potatoes, lima beans, parsnips, pumpkin and winter squash are particularly good sources of potassium. Starchy vegetables are included here because they contain the same amount of carbohydrate and protein as one slice of bread. This list shows the kinds and amounts of breads, cereals, starchy vegetables and prepared foods to use for one Bread Exchange.

Bread
White, including French
and Italian . . . . 1 slice
Whole wheat . . . . 1 slice
Rye or pumpernickel . . . . 1 slice
Raisin . . . . 1 slice
Bagel, small . . . . ½
English muffin, small . . . . ½
Plain roll, bread 1
Frankfurter roll . . . . ½
Hamburger bun . . . . ½
Dried bread crumbs . . . . 3 tablespoons
Tortilla, 6-in.
diameter 1
Sour dough bread . . . . 1 slice
Croutons . . . . ½ cup
Holland rusk . . . . 2 average
Popover . . . . 1 average
Bread sticks, thin,
9-in. long 4

Cereal
Bran . . . . ⅓ cup
Bran flakes . . . . ½ cup
Other ready-to-eat
unsweetened cereal . . . . ¾ cup
Puffed cereal, unfrosted . . . . . 1 cup
Cereal — cooked . . . . ½ cup
Grits — cooked . . . . ½ cup
Grapenuts . . . . 3 tablespoons
Shredded wheat . . . . 1 large biscuit
Wheat germ . . . . ¼ cup
Matzo farfel . . . . 7 tablespoons

Flours
Arrowroot . . . . 2 tablespoons
All-purpose . . . . 2½ tablespoons
Bran, unprocessed . . . . 5 tablespoons
Cake . . . . 2½ tablespoons
Cornmeal . . . . 2 tablespoons
Cornstarch . . . . 2 tablespoons
Matzo meal . . . . 3 tablespoons
Rye . . . . 4 tablespoons
Whole wheat . . . . 3 tablespoons
Bulgar . . . . 1½ tablespoons
Potato flour . . . . 2½ tablespoons

Pasta — cooked
Noodles . . . . ½ cup
Spaghetti . . . . ½ cup
Macaroni . . . . ½ cup

Starchy Vegetables
Corn . . . . ⅓ cup
Corn on the cob . . . . 1 small
Lima Beans . . . . ½ cup
Parsnips . . . . ⅔ cup
Peas, green —
canned or frozen . . . . ½ cup
Potato, white . . . . 1 small
Potato, mashed . . . . ½ cup
Pumpkin . . . . ¾ cup
Winter squash, acorn
or butternut . . . . ½ cup
Yam or sweet potato . . . . ¼ cup
Chick peas or
garbanzo beans . . . . ¼ cup
Dried beans, peas,
lentils — cooked . . . . ½ cup
Baked beans, no pork
— canned . . . . ¼ cup
Rice, brown — cooked . . . . ⅓ cup
Rice, white — cooked . . . . ½ cup
Barley — cooked . . . . ½ cup
Wild rice — cooked . . . . 3 tablespoons

Crackers
Arrowroot 3
Graham, 2½-in. squares 2
Matzo, 4 × 6-in 1½
Oyster 20
Pretzels, 3⅛-in. long,
⅛-in. diameter 25
Rye wafers, 2 × 3½-in. 3
Saltines 6
Soda, 2½-in. square 4
Pilot crackers 1
Waverly wafers 6
Crackers, crushed . . . . ¼ cup
Cracker meal, coarse . . . . ⅓ cup
Graham cracker crumbs . . . . . 3 tablespoons
Zwieback 3
Lorna Doone Shortbread 3
Vanilla wafers 5

Bread Exchanges (continued)

The following contain 1 additional Fat Exchange and a total of 115 calories.

Biscuit, 2-in. diameter*	1
Corn bread, 2 × 2 × 1-in.*	1
Corn muffin, 2-in. diameter	1
Crackers, round butter type*	5
Muffin, plain, small*	1
Potatoes, French fried, 2 to 3½-in.*	8
Pancake, 5 × ½-in.*	1
Waffle, 5 × ½-in.*	1

The following contain 2 additional Fat Exchanges and a total of 160 calories.

Potato or corn chips*	15
Ice cream**	½ cup

Miscellaneous

Cocktail sauce	4 tablespoons
Popcorn, popped, no fat added	3 cups
Tapioca, granulated	2 tablespoons

*cholesterol content will depend on type of fat used.
**high cholesterol item.

Fat Exchanges: One Fat Exchange contains 45 calories and 5 grams of fat.

Fats are of both animal and vegetable origin. Margarine, butter, cream and cream cheese contain vitamin A. This list shows the kinds and amounts of fat-containing foods to use for one Fat Exchange.

Avocado, 4 in. diameter	⅛
Bacon fat*	1 teaspoon
Bacon, crisp*	1 strip
Butter*	1 teaspoon
Butter, whipped*	2 teaspoons
Cream, sour*	2 tablespoons
Half and Half*	2 tablespoons
Half and Half, sour*	3 tablespoons
Cream, heavy*	1 tablespoon
Cream, whipped, heavy*	2 tablespoons
Cream cheese*	1 tablespoon
Lard*	1 teaspoon

Margarine, regular stick**	1 teaspoon
Margarine, soft, tub or stick**	1 teaspoon
Margarine, diet**	2 teaspoons

Nuts

Almonds	6 nuts
Brazil nuts	2 medium
Cashews	3 to 4
Filberts	5
Macadamia	4 halves
Mixed	4 to 6
Peanuts, Virginia	10
Peanuts, Spanish	20
Pecans	2 large whole
Pistachio	20
Sunflower seeds	1½ tablespoons
Sunflower kernels	1 tablespoon
Walnuts	6 small
Sesame seeds	1 tablespoon

Oil

Corn, cotton seed, safflower, soybean, sunflower	1 teaspoon
Olive	1 teaspoon
Peanut	1 teaspoon

Olives	5 small

Salad dressings***

Blue cheese	2 teaspoons
French	1 tablespoon
Italian	1 tablespoon
Mayonnaise	1 teaspoon
Salad dressing, mayonnaise type	2 teaspoons

Salt Pork	¾-in. cube

*Indicates high cholesterol item.
**Made with corn, cottonseed, safflower, soybean or sunflower oil only.
***If made with corn, cottonseed, safflower, soybean or sunflower oil can be used on fat modified diet.

Meat Exchanges: One **Low Fat Meat Exchange** contains 55 calories, 7 grams of protein, and 3 grams of fat.

All the foods here are good sources of protein and many are also good sources of iron, zinc, vitamin B$_{12}$ and other vitamins of the vitamin B-complex. Cholesterol is of animal origin. Foods of plant origin have no cholesterol. Oysters are outstanding for their high zinc content. Other good sources of zinc are crab, liver, trimmed lean meat, dark turkey meat, dried beans and peas and peanut butter. Particularly good sources of magnesium and potassium include dried beans, peas and peanut butter. This list shows the kinds and amounts of lean meat and other protein-rich foods to use for one Low Fat Meat Exchange. Trim off all visible fat.

Beef
    Baby beef (very lean), chipped beef, chuck, flank steak, tenderloin, plate ribs, plate skirt steak, round (bottom, top), all cuts rump, spare ribs, tripe . . 1 oz.

Lamb
    Leg, rib, sirloin, loin (roast and chops), shank, shoulder . . . . 1 oz.

Pork
    Leg (whole rump, center shank), ham, smoked (center slices). . . . . 1 oz.

Poultry-skinned
    Chicken, turkey, Cornish game hen, Guinea hen, pheasant . . . . 1 oz.

Veal
    Leg, loin, rib, shank, shoulder, cutlets . . . . 1 oz.

Fish
    Any fresh, frozen or canned salmon, tuna, mackerel. . . . . 1 oz.
    Crab and lobster. . . . . ¼ cup
    Clams, oysters, scallops, shrimp . . . . . 5 or 1 oz.
    Sardines, drained 3

Cheese
    Cheeses containing less than 5% butterfat. . . . . 1 oz.
    Cottage cheese, dry and 2% butterfat . . . . ¼ cup

One **Medium Fat Exchange** contains 78 calories, 7 grams of protein and 5.5 grams of fat. This list shows the kinds and amounts of medium fat meat and other protein rich foods to use for one Medium Fat Meat Exchange. All items on this list except peanut butter are high in cholesterol. Trim off all visible fat.

Beef
    Ground (15% fat), corned beef (canned), rib eye, round (ground commercial). . . . . 1 oz.

Pork
    Loin (all cuts tenderloin), shoulder arm (picnic), shoulder blade, Boston butt, Canadian bacon, boiled ham . . . 1 oz.

Liver, heart, kidney, sweet breads (these are high in cholesterol) . . . . 1 oz.

Cheese
    Cottage cheese, creamed (over 5% butterfat) . . . . ¼ cup
    Neufchâtel, ricotta, farmer's cheese, mozzarella . . . . 1 oz.
    Parmesan (over 5% butterfat). . . . . . . 3 tbsp.

Egg (high in cholesterol). 1

Peanut butter
    (this has 2 additional fat exchanges and a total of 168 calories) . . . . 2 tbsp.

One **High Fat Meat Exchange** contains 100 calories, 7 grams of protein and 8 grams of fat. This list shows the kinds and amounts of high fat meat and other protein rich foods to use for one High Fat Meat Exchange. All items on this list are high in cholesterol. Trim off all visible fat.

Beef
    Brisket, corned beef (brisket), ground beef (more than 20% fat), hamburger (commercial), chuck (ground commercial), roasts (rib), steaks, (club and rib). . . . . 1 oz.

Lamb
    Breast . . . . 1 oz.

Pork
    Spare ribs, loin (back ribs), pork (ground), country style ham, deviled ham . . . . 1 oz.

Veal
    Breast . . . . 1 oz.

Poultry
    Capon, duck (domestic), goose . . . . . 1 oz.

Cheese
    Cheddar types. . . . . 1 oz.

Cold cuts . . . . 4½ × ⅛-in. slice

Frankfurter . . . . 1 small

Sausage . . . . 1 oz.

Free Foods: Free foods are 20 calories or less per serving.

Free foods are not altered in any way, such as omitting or replacing sugar. Some seasonings and beverages (coffee and tea) are allowed freely because they cannot actually be considered food, since they provide no nourishment.

Beverages

Coffee
Tea
Sanka
Sugar-free soda pop
Powdered soft drink mix with
  no sugar added

Sauces

A-1 sauce*
Catsup (1 tablespoon)*
Chili sauce (1 tablespoon)*
Tabasco sauce
Worcestershire sauce (1 tablespoon)*

Seasonings

Allspice
Angostura bitters
Anise
Basil
Bay leaf
Caraway
Cardamon
Celery salt or seed
Chervil
Chili powder
Chives
Cinnamon
Cloves
Cocoa powder—limit
  to 2 teaspoons
Cumin
Curry
Extracts, vanilla, etc.
Garlic, whole, salt or
  powder
Horseradish
Lemon or
  orange rind
Lemon or lime
  juice—limit to 2
  teaspoons per day
Mace
Marjoram
Mint
Mustard, dry or
  prepared
Nutmeg
Onion, salt or
  powder
Oregano
Paprika
Parsley
Pepper, black or
  cayenne
Poppy seed
Poultry seasoning
Rosemary
Saffron
Sage
Salt
Tenderizers
Thyme
Vinegar

Soups

Consommé, without fat*
Bouillon, without fat*
Clear broth*
Soups/broth made with foods on this list*

Vegetables-raw

Alfalfa sprouts
Celery cabbage
Chard
Chicory
Cilantro (coriander
  leaf)
Dandelion
Endive
Escarole
Lettuce
Mushrooms
Mustard greens
Radishes
Romaine lettuce
Spinach
Watercress
Zucchini

Miscellaneous

Sour pickles*
Some kinds of pickle relish*
Dill pickles or other unsweetened pickles*
Cranberries, unsweetened
Low calorie salad dressings*
  (no more than 20 calories per serving)
Non-dairy whipped topping
  (1 tablespoon)

*Contains sodium

Making Foods Taste Good

Most of us grew up adding salt and butter to our food to improve flavor. When we diet, we need to find new ways of seasoning. The microwave oven helps, because it brings out the natural flavor of foods and allows you to cook fat-free, so your daily fat allowance can be used, instead, in the form of nuts, avocado or salad dressing.

In this section you'll find recipes for seasoning mixtures you can keep on hand to vary the taste of food, plus an herb and spice chart to guide you in experimenting with new flavors.

Seasoning alters the character of a dish dramatically. Be sparing with herbs and spices added to food before cooking because microwaving intensifies their flavors, too.

Herb Salt

½ cup table salt
2 tablespoons parsley flakes
2 tablespoons tarragon leaves
2 tablespoons dry chopped
  chives
2 tablespoons savory

Makes 1½ cups
Serving size: ¼ teaspoon

Combine all ingredients in small bowl. Store in tightly closed jar. Serve with fish and seafood, poultry, eggs, salads and assorted vegetables.

NOTE: for low sodium diet use salt substitute. Fresh chopped herbs may be substituted for the dried. Double the amount.

Per Serving:
  Calories: 0
  Sodium: 168 mg.
  Cholesterol: 0
  Exchanges: free

Herb Pepper

¼ cup black pepper
1 tablespoon dried thyme
1 tablespoon caraway seed
1 tablespoon paprika
1 teaspoon garlic powder
1 tablespoon sesame seed

Makes ½ cup
Serving size: ¼ teaspoon

Mix all ingredients together. Store in tightly closed jar. Serve with roasts and broiled meats.

Per Serving:
  Calories: 0
  Sodium: 0
  Cholesterol: 0
  Exchanges: free

Seasoned Bread Crumbs

1 cup fine bread crumbs
¼ cup Parmesan or shredded
  Cheddar cheese
½ teaspoon garlic powder
1 tablespoon vegetable oil
2 tablespoons fresh snipped
  parsley or 1 tablespoon
  parsley flakes
½ teaspoon table salt
¼ teaspoon black pepper

Makes 1½ cups
Serving size: ¼ cup

Combine all ingredients. Store in tightly closed container. Mixture keeps best in freezer, but will keep for one week in refrigerator.

Serve as topping for casseroles and assorted vegetables, or as coating for chicken, pork chops or veal.

NOTE: for low sodium diet use salt substitute.

Per Serving:
  Calories: 92
  Sodium: 324 mg.
  Cholesterol: 13 mg.
  Exchanges: 1 bread, ½ fat

Dill Salt

½ cup table salt
¾ cup dill weed

Makes 1¼ cups
Serving size: ¼ teaspoon

Combine salt and dill. Store in tightly closed jar.

Serve with fish and seafood, salads, cucumbers, string beans and assorted vegetables.

NOTE: for low sodium diet use salt substitute.

Per Serving:
  Calories: 0
  Sodium: 200 mg.
  Cholesterol: 0
  Exchanges: free

Seasoned Salt

¼ cup table salt
1 tablespoon paprika
1 teaspoon black pepper
1 teaspoon onion powder
½ teaspoon garlic powder
1 teaspoon dry mustard
1 teaspoon allspice
1 teaspoon coriander
  Dash nutmeg

Makes ⅔ cup
Serving size: ¼ teaspoon

Blend all ingredients well. Store in tightly closed jar. Serve with beef, veal, eggs and salads.

NOTE: for low sodium diet use salt substitute.

Per Serving:
  Calories: 0
  Sodium: 160 mg.
  Cholesterol: 0
  Exchanges: free

All-Purpose Herb Blend

1 tablespoon garlic powder
1 teaspoon black pepper
1 tablespoon dried oregano
1 tablespoon parsley flakes
1 tablespoon dried basil

Makes ¼ cup
Serving size: ¼ teaspoon

Blend all ingredients well. Store in tightly closed jar. Serve with poultry, broiled meats, roasts, salads and assorted vegetables.

NOTE: Fresh chopped herbs may be substituted for the dried. Double the amount.

Per Serving:
  Calories: 0
  Sodium: 0
  Cholesterol: 0
  Exchanges: free

Herbs & Spices Chart

Spice	Meat	Poultry	Fish & Seafood	Eggs & Cheese	Vegetables	Sauces	Desserts
Allspice	Ham Meatballs Meat Loaf Pot Roast Spare Ribs Stew	Chicken Fricassee	Steamed Fish		Carrots Eggplant Potato Soup Spinach Squash Turnips	Barbecue Cranberry Tomato	Fruitcake Fruits Mince Pie Pumpkin Pie Steamed Pudding
Basil	Beef Lamb Pork Veal	Chicken	Crab Shrimp Steamed Fish Tuna	Creamed Eggs Omelets Scrambled Eggs Soufflés	Bean Soup Eggplant Green Beans Tomatoes Wax Beans Potato Soup	Spaghetti Tomato	
Bay Leaf	Soups Stews Tongue	Chicken Chicken Soup Chicken Stew	Shrimp		Artichokes Beets Green Beans Tomatoes	Gravies Marinades	
Caraway Seed	Pork		Fish Seafood Stew	Cottage Cheese	Cabbage Potatoes Sauerkraut	Cheese	
Celery Seed	Stews		Fish	Cheese Dishes	Cabbage Cauliflower Onions Potato Salad Tomatoes		
Chili Powder	Beef Stew Chili Tamales	Barbecued Chicken Chicken	Shrimp	Fondue Scrambled Eggs	Cauliflower Lima Beans Onions Pea Soup	Cheese Seafood	
Cinnamon	Beef Stew Ham Pork	Stewed Chicken	Shrimp		Carrots Onions Spinach Squash Sweet Potatoes	Apple	Apples Fruit Compotes Puddings
Cloves	Ham Soups Stews Tongue	Creamed Chicken	Fish		Bean Soup Beets Carrots Onions Squash	Tomato	Apples Gingerbread Pears
Coriander	Curries Meatballs Meat Loaf Sausage	Curries	Curries				Apple Pie Peach Pie Rice Pudding
Cumin	Chili Curry Sausage Soups Stews		Curries	Egg Dishes Cheese Dishes	Sauerkraut Tomatoes		
Dill Seed Dill Weed	Beef Lamb Pork Soups Stews Veal	Chicken	Salmon Shellfish	Cottage Cheese Deviled Eggs	Beans Cabbage Carrots Cauliflower Lentils Peas Potatoes	Cocktail Sauce Fish	

Spice	Meat	Poultry	Fish & Seafood	Eggs & Cheese	Vegetables	Sauces	Desserts

Ginger	Beef
	Pork
	Pot Roast
		Roast
		  Chicken
		Stir Fries
			Fish	Macaroni
				  & Cheese
					Baked Beans
					Beets
					Carrots
					Squash
					Sweet Potatoes
							Gingerbread
							Pears
							Puddings
							Steamed Fruit

Mace & Nutmeg	Meatballs Meat Loaf Pot Roast Stews Veal Soups	Chicken Fricassee	Fish Oysters Shrimp Creole	Quiche Lorraine	Artichokes Brussels Sprouts Cabbage Onions Spinach	Cheese Fish Mushroom Spaghetti	Apple Pie Custard Pumpkin Pie

Marjoram	Beef
	Lamb
	Liver
	Meatballs
	Meat Loaf
	Pork
	Stews
	Veal
		Chicken
		  Salad
		Roast
		  Chicken
		Soups
		Stuffings
		Turkey
			Crab
			Salmon
				Cheese
				  Soufflé
				Omelets
				Scrambled
				  Eggs
					Celery
					Eggplant
					Green Beans
					Lima Beans
					Onion Soup
					Potatoes
					Spinach
					Zucchini		

Oregano	Chili Hamburger Liver Pot Roast Soups Stews Veal	Chicken	Fish Shellfish		Broccoli Cabbage Eggplant Lentils Onions Tomatoes Onions Zucchini	Mushroom Spaghetti	

Parsley	Meat Loaf
	Pot Roast
	Soups
	Stews
		Stuffings	Fish Fillets
			Lobster
				Cottage
				  Cheese
				Scrambled
				  Eggs
					Beans
					Carrots
					Cauliflower
					Eggplant
					Mushrooms
					Peas
					Potatoes
					Tomatoes
						Spaghetti	

Rosemary	Beef
	Lamb
	Pork
	Veal
		Roast
		  Chicken
		Roast
		  Turkey
		Stuffings
			Fish Fillets	Egg Dishes
				Cheese
				  Dishes
					Eggplant
					Mushrooms
					Onions		

Sage	Ham
	Pork
	Sausage
	Veal
		Roast
		  Chicken
		Roast
		  Turkey
		Soups
		Stuffings
			Fish	Cheese
				  Dishes
				Cottage
				  Cheese
				Egg Dishes
					Brussels
					  Sprouts
					Egg Plant
					Green Beans
					Lima Beans
					Squash
					Tomatoes
						Cheese	

Tarragon	Beef Veal	Chicken	Fish Fillets Lobster	Egg Dishes	Beets Spinach	Fish	

Thyme	Beef
	Lamb
	Pork
	Soups
	Stews
		Chicken
		Stuffings
			Clam
			  Chowder
			Oysters
			Tuna
				Omelets
				Scrambled
				  Eggs
				Soufflés
					Carrots
					Eggplant
					Green Beans
					Onions
					Peas
					Tomatoes		

Menu Planning

When you're planning diet menus, consider the day as a whole, rather than planning one meal at a time. Divide your daily calorie, sodium or cholesterol allowance between three meals, and include each of the major food groups some time during the day. While a big breakfast is not necessary, at least one-fifth of your daily calorie allowance should be consumed in the morning. It's a good idea to divide the remaining calories evenly between lunch and dinner. If you follow a small breakfast with a light lunch, you may be so hungry by late afternoon that you can't resist a snack, or you eat more for dinner than your diet allows. Your daily menu should include protein, vegetables, fruit, bread, and a calcium source. If you follow an exchange diet, your nutrition will be balanced between these groups automatically.

Breakfast Menus

Carrot Bran Muffins, page 138
Citrus Warmer, page 41
Spiced Yogurt Omelet,
  page 107

Microwave Carrot Bran Muffins. Microwave Citrus Warmer. Let stand, covered, while microwaving Spiced Yogurt Omelet. If desired, reheat muffins at High 1 minute.

Total Meal — One Serving:
Calories:	223
Sodium:	242 mg.
Cholesterol:	268 mg.
Exchanges:	1½ fruit, 1 bread, 1 med. fat meat, 1 fat

Raisin Orange Muffins,
page 138
Baked Pears, page 151
Santa Fe Scrambled Eggs,
page 109

Microwave Raisin Orange
Muffins. Set aside. Microwave
Baked Pears. Microwave Santa
Fe Scrambled Eggs. Let stand
while reheating muffins at High
1 minute.

Total Meal — One Serving:	
Calories:	269
Sodium:	387 mg.
Cholesterol:	297 mg.
Exchanges:	½ vegetable,
	1 fruit, 1 bread,
	1 med. fat meat,
	½ fat

Wheat Biscuits, page 136
Breakfast Soufflé, page 105
Baked Grapefruit, page 126

Microwave Wheat Biscuits.
Assemble Baked Grapefruit. Set
aside. Microwave Breakfast
Soufflé. If desired, reheat
biscuits at High 1 minute.
Microwave grapefruit
immediately before serving.

Total Meal — One Serving:	
Calories:	240
Sodium:	428 mg.
Cholesterol:	127 mg.
Exchanges:	1½ fruit, 1 bread,
	1 med. fat meat,
	½ fat

Lunch Menus

Crustless Ricotta Pie, page 106
Crab Stuffed Cherry Tomatoes,
  page 27

Prepare filling and stuff cherry
tomatoes. Microwave Crustless
Ricotta Pie. Let stand while
microwaving Crab Stuffed
Cherry Tomatoes.

Total Meal — One Serving:
  Calories: 141
  Sodium: 382 mg.
  Cholesterol: 82 mg.
  Exchanges: 2 vegetable, 1 low
                 fat meat, ½ med.
                 fat meat

Burgers With Mushroom Sauce,
  page 49
Crunchy Asparagus, page 115
Peach Melba, page 145

Microwave peach halves. Let
cool. Microwave Burgers With
Mushroom Sauce. Let stand,
covered, while microwaving
Crunchy Asparagus. Top
peaches with jam and complete
microwaving before serving.

Total Meal — One Serving:
  Calories: 322
  Sodium: 586 mg.
  Cholesterol: 77 mg.
  Exchanges: 2 vegetable, 2 fruit,
                 3 low fat meat

Spiced Coffee, page 39
Taco Dinner Salad, page 52
Chocolate Mint Tapioca
  Pudding, page 150

Prepare Chocolate Mint Tapioca
Pudding ahead. Refrigerate.
Microwave Spiced Coffee.
Prepare Taco Salad.

Total Meal — One Serving:
  Calories: 315
  Sodium: 560 mg.
  Cholesterol: 89 mg.
  Exchanges: ½ milk, 1½
                 vegetable, 1 fruit,
                 3 low fat meat,
                 ½ med. fat meat

Mexican Pizza Sandwich,
  page 36
Lemon Cheesecake, page 142

Microwave Lemon Cheesecake
and refrigerate. Microwave
Mexican Pizza Sandwich.

Total Meal — One Serving:
  Calories: 311
  Sodium: 189 mg.
  Cholesterol: 164 mg.
  Exchanges: 1 vegetable, 1 fruit,
                 1 bread, 2½ med.
                 fat meat

Dinner Menus

Stuffed Celery (2 pieces),
  page 26
Sole Florentine, page 95
Salad with low calorie
  dressing, page 13
Ginger Peach Parfait, page 150

Prepare Ginger Peach Parfait
ahead. Refrigerate. Prepare
celery stuffing. While microwaving Sole Florentine, assemble Stuffed Celery and a salad
of "free" vegetables from the
Free Exchange List.

Total Meal — One Serving:
  Calories: 336
  Sodium: 390 mg.
  Cholesterol: 70 mg.
  Exchanges: 2 vegetable, 1 fruit,
                   1 bread, 2 low fat
                   meat, ½ high
                   fat meat

Egg Drop Soup, page 33
Turkey Chow Mein, page 77
Hot Strawberry Ambrosia,
  page 142

Assemble Hot Strawberry
Ambrosia. Set aside. Prepare
and microwave Turkey Chow
Mein; omit noodles. Let stand,
covered, while microwaving Egg
Drop Soup. If necessary, reheat
Chow Mein at High 1 to 3
minutes. Top with noodles and
serve. Microwave Strawberry
Ambrosia just before serving.

Total Meal — One Serving:
  Calories: 292
  Sodium: 1005 mg.
  Cholesterol: 55 mg.
  Exchanges: 2 vegetable, 2 fruit,
                   ½ bread, 2 low fat
                   meat, ½ fat

Minestrone, page 31
Mushroom Veal, page 61
Baked Potato, page 121
  with 2 tablespoons sour cream
Tropical Chiffon, page 143

Prepare Tropical Chiffon ahead.
Refrigerate. Microwave potatoes; wrap in foil and let stand.
Assemble Mushroom Veal while
microwaving Minestrone. Let
soup stand, covered, while
microwaving veal.

Total Meal — One Serving:
  Calories: 361
  Sodium: 592 mg.
  Cholesterol: 155 mg.
  Exchanges: 2 vegetable, 1 fruit,
                1 bread, 3½ low
                fat meat

Hot Bouillon, page 40
Fruit Stuffed Chicken, page 78
Salad with low calorie
  dressing, page 13
Mocha Crêpe, page 147

Prepare crêpes ahead. Prepare
crêpe filling. Set aside.
Microwave Fruit Stuffed
Chicken. Let stand, covered.
While microwaving Hot Bouillon,
prepare a salad of "free"
vegetables from the Free
Exchange List. Assemble
crêpes before serving.

Total Meal — One Serving:
  Calories: 372
  Sodium: 1145 mg.
  Cholesterol: 105 mg.
  Exchanges: 1 fruit, 1 bread,
                3 med. fat meat,
                ½ fat

Appetizers

This collection of good tasting, low calorie appetizers is for the enjoyment of dieters and non-dieters alike. When entertaining, you can join your guests in sampling the hors d'oeuvres.

With dips or spreads, offer a selection of crisp, fresh vegetables. Microwaving offers an alternative to strictly raw vegetables. Microwave raw vegetables at High about one minute per cup, or until heated, stirring once. Chill until serving time. This cuts the raw taste without destroying the crispness.

Liver Paté

1 lb. chicken livers, rinsed and drained
2 cloves garlic, minced
1 small onion, chopped
2 tablespoons white wine or water
½ teaspoon parsley flakes
½ teaspoon salt, optional
½ teaspoon pepper
1 hard cooked egg, chopped
1 tablespoon brandy

Serves 16
Serving size: 2 tablespoons

In 2-qt. casserole combine livers, garlic, onion, wine and seasonings; cover. Microwave at High 5 to 8 minutes, or until meat is no longer pink, stirring once. Drain well.

Place cooked livers, egg and brandy in blender or food processor. Puree until smooth. Turn into serving dish and chill.

Pipe or spoon paté on melba toast, cherry tomatoes or celery sticks.

Per Serving:
Calories: 62
Sodium: 82 mg.
Cholesterol: 173 mg.
Exchanges: 1 low fat meat

Clam Dip

½ pkg. (8 oz.) Neufchâtel cheese
1 can (6½ oz.) minced clams, drained
¼ cup plain low fat yogurt
¼ cup chopped onion
1 teaspoon prepared horseradish
1 teaspoon Worcestershire sauce

Serves 10
Serving size: 2 tablespoons

Place cheese in small baking dish. Microwave at 50% (Medium) 45 seconds to 1¼ minutes, stirring after half the time. Stir in remaining ingredients. Microwave at 50% (Medium) 3½ to 5½ minutes, or until heated through, stirring after half the cooking time.

Serve hot or cold with assorted fresh vegetables.

Per Serving:
Calories: 56
Sodium: 16 mg.
Cholesterol: 9 mg.
Exchanges: 1 low fat meat

◄ Marinated Vegetables

1 cup tomato juice
½ cup water
½ cup thinly sliced celery
1 teaspoon onion powder
½ teaspoon basil leaves
½ teaspoon oregano leaves
¼ teaspoon garlic powder
⅛ teaspoon tarragon leaves
1 cup cauliflowerets
1 cup broccoli flowerets
1 cup thin carrot strips

Serves 8

Combine tomato juice, water, celery, onion powder, basil, oregano, garlic powder, and tarragon in 2-qt. casserole. Microwave at High 3 to 5 minutes, or until bubbly.

Stir in vegetables. Microwave at High 3 minutes. Reduce power to (50%) Medium. Microwave 3 to 5 minutes, or until flavors are blended and vegetables are softened. Serve warm or chilled.

NOTE: for low sodium diet, use low sodium tomato juice.

Per Serving:
Calories: 23
Sodium: 65 mg.
Cholesterol: 0
Exchanges: 1 vegetable

Stuffed Celery ▲

2 tablespoons assorted dry
   vegetable flakes
½ teaspoon onion flakes
3 tablespoons water
2 oz. Neufchâtel cheese
4 large celery stalks,
   ends trimmed
Paprika

Serves 10
Serving size: 2 pieces

In 1-cup measure combine vegetable flakes, onion flakes and water. Cover with plastic wrap. Microwave at High 20 to 45 seconds, or until vegetable flakes are soft. Set aside.

Place cheese in small bowl. Reduce power to 50% (Medium). Microwave 20 to 45 seconds, or until softened. Stir in vegetable flakes.

Stuff celery with cheese mixture. Cut each stalk into 5 pieces. Sprinkle with paprika.

Per Serving:
Calories: 18
Sodium: 1 mg.
Cholesterol: 1 mg.
Exchanges: free

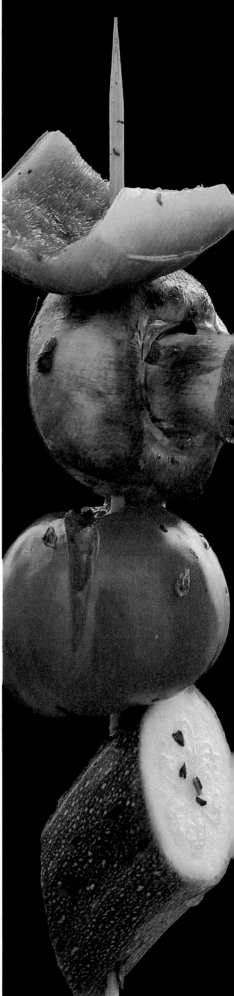

Crab Stuffed Cherry▲ Tomatoes

1 pint cherry tomatoes
1 can (5 oz.) crab meat,
   rinsed and drained,
   cartilage removed
2 green onions, finely chopped
1 teaspoon white wine vinegar
¼ cup finely chopped green
   pepper
½ teaspoon parsley flakes
¼ teaspoon dill weed, optional
2 tablespoons seasoned dry
   bread crumbs
   Paprika

Serves 5
Serving size: 5 tomatoes

Cut stem end from tomatoes and scoop out pulp. Set aside. Combine remaining ingredients except paprika in small mixing bowl. Stuff tomatoes with crab mixture. Place tomatoes on paper towel-lined plate, with smaller tomatoes toward center. Microwave at High 2 to 4 minutes, or until heated through, rotating plate once or twice. Sprinkle with paprika.

NOTE: for low sodium diets, substitute well-drained frozen crab meat.

Per Serving:
   Calories: 80
   Sodium: 282 mg.
   Cholesterol: 16 mg.
   Exchanges: 1 vegetable, 1 low
                   fat meat

Vegetable Kabobs ►

8 wooden skewers, 6-in. long
8 green pepper chunks, 1-in.
8 large fresh mushrooms
8 cherry tomatoes
8 zucchini chunks, 1-in.
½ cup boiling water
½ teaspoon instant beef
   bouillon granules
¼ cup white wine
¼ teaspoon salt, optional
¼ teaspoon thyme leaves
¼ teaspoon marjoram
⅛ teaspoon black pepper
1 bay leaf

Serves 8

On each of the 8 skewers place 1 pepper chunk, mushroom, tomato and zucchini chunk.

In 12 × 8-in. baking dish blend water and bouillon. Stir in wine and seasonings. Add kabobs and turn to coat. Cover dish with wax paper. Let stand in refrigerator 2 to 3 hours, turning once or twice. Discard marinade. Place kabobs on roasting rack. Microwave at High 4 to 7 minutes, or until vegetables are tender-crisp, turning over and rearranging after half the time.

Per Serving:
   Calories: 15
   Sodium: 58 mg.
   Cholesterol: 0
   Exchanges: ½ vegetable

Sweet & Sour Chicken Wings ▲

2 lbs. chicken wings
¼ cup white wine vinegar
1 tablespoon honey
1 tablespoon soy sauce
1 tablespoon catsup

½ teaspoon ginger
1 can (8 oz.) chunk pineapple,
  packed in own juice
½ teaspoon bouquet sauce

Serves 12
Serving size: 2 wings

Cut chicken wings into 3 pieces, separating at joints. Discard wing tips. Combine remaining ingredients and wing pieces in plastic bag or small bowl. Let stand overnight, turning wings once or twice. Place marinade and chicken wings in 8 × 8-in. dish. Cover with wax paper. Microwave at High 8 to 12 minutes, or until chicken wings are fork tender, stirring once during cooking.

NOTE: for low sodium diet substitute low-salt soy sauce and catsup.

Per Serving:
Calories: 71   Cholesterol: 58 mg.
Sodium: 105 mg.   Exchanges: ½ fruit, 1 low fat meat

Chicken Kabobs ▲

12 wooden skewers, 6-in. long
1 whole boneless chicken
  breast, skin removed, cut
  into 24 pieces
1 medium green pepper,
  cut into 24 pieces
1 apple, cut into 24 pieces
1 teaspoon lemon juice
1 tablespoon water
1 teaspoon lemon pepper

Serves 4
Serving size: 3 kabobs

On each skewer alternate 1 piece of chicken, green pepper and apple; repeat once. Place on roasting rack. Combine lemon juice with water; brush on kabobs. Sprinkle with lemon pepper. Cover with wax paper. Microwave at 50% (Medium) 8 to 12 minutes, or until chicken is no longer pink, rearranging and basting once or twice.

Per Serving:
Calories: 21
Sodium: 11 mg.
Cholesterol: 13 mg.
Exchanges: free

Gingered Meatballs ▲

Meatballs:
1 lb. extra lean ground beef
3 green onions, chopped
1 egg, slightly beaten
1 teaspoon ground ginger
⅛ teaspoon garlic powder

Sauce:
½ cup water
2 teaspoons cornstarch
1 tablespoon soy sauce
1 teaspoon white wine
  vinegar
2 teaspoons parsley flakes

Serves 12
Serving size: 3 meatballs

Combine meatball ingredients in medium mixing bowl. Blend thoroughly. Form meatballs using 2 level teaspoons of meat for each. Place meatballs in 12 × 8-in. baking dish. Microwave at High 4 to 7 minutes, or until meatballs are no longer pink, turning once or twice during cooking. Remove meatballs from dish. Set aside.

Combine water and cornstarch in 1-cup measure. Blend into meat juices in baking dish; add soy sauce, vinegar, and parsley flakes. Microwave at High 4 to 7 minutes, or until thickened and bubbly, stirring once or twice. Pour sauce over meatballs. Microwave at High 1 to 3 minutes, or until heated through.

Per Serving:
  Calories: 60   Cholesterol: 43 mg.
  Sodium: 103 mg.   Exchanges: 1 low fat meat

Spicy Shrimp ▲

1 pkg. (10 oz.) frozen medium
  size cleaned shrimp,
  defrosted, rinsed, drained
¼ cup white wine
1 clove garlic, pressed or
  minced
½ teaspoon parsley flakes
⅛ teaspoon salt, optional
⅛ teaspoon black pepper
⅛ teaspoon tarragon
  Dash red pepper flakes
1 small bay leaf

Serves 5

Combine all ingredients in 2-qt. casserole. Cover with wax paper. Microwave at High 3½ to 6 minutes, or until shrimp are opaque, stirring after half the time. Let stand 3 to 5 minutes.

Per Serving:
  Calories: 114
  Sodium: 96 mg.
  Cholesterol: 85 mg.
  Exchanges: 2 low fat meat

Soups

A low calorie soup, savored slowly, is a smart way to start a meal. It takes the edge off your appetite and helps you feel full. Soup, combined with a salad of "free foods" to provide bulk, makes a satisfying lunch. These recipes are low calorie versions of some of your favorite soups—Chicken Noodle, Split Pea and Tomato. You can microwave them quickly and easily without all day simmering.

Minestrone

½ cup thinly sliced celery
½ cup thinly sliced carrot
2 cloves garlic, minced
¾ cup (1 large) potato, cut
  into ½-in. cubes
1 can (16 oz.) tomatoes,
  undrained
1 cup thinly sliced zucchini
½ lb. green beans, cut into
  1-in. pieces
½ cup broken spaghetti
3 cups hot water
2 teaspoons instant beef
  bouillon granules
1 teaspoon basil leaves
1 tablespoon parsley flakes

Serves 6

In 3-qt. casserole, combine all ingredients. Cover. Microwave at High 25 to 35 minutes or until vegetables are tender, stirring once or twice.

NOTE: for low sodium diet substitute low-salt bouillon.

Per Serving:	
Calories:	35
Sodium:	315 mg.
Cholesterol:	0
Exchanges:	1½ vegetable

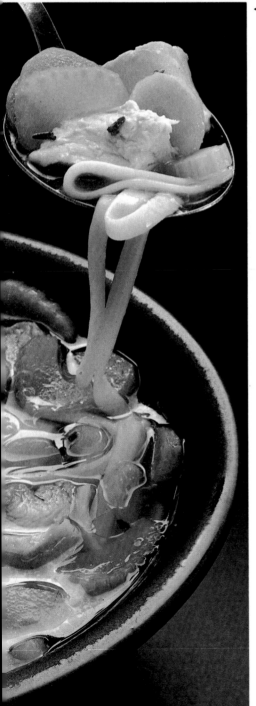

◄ Chicken Noodle Soup

2½ to 3 lbs. chicken pieces
6 cups hot water, divided
2 large stalks celery, thinly
　sliced
2 medium carrots, thinly
　sliced
½ teaspoon dried basil
¼ teaspoon rosemary
¼ teaspoon pepper
1 teaspoon salt, optional
½ cup thin egg noodles

Serves 8

In 5-qt. casserole combine
chicken, 4 cups water, celery,
carrots, basil, rosemary, pepper
and salt; cover. Microwave at
High 30 to 40 minutes, or until
chicken falls easily from bone,
stirring twice during cooking.

Remove chicken from bones.
Discard bone and skin. Dice
meat and return to casserole.
Add 2 cups hot water and
noodles. Cover. Microwave at
High 8 to 10 minutes, or until
water boils. Microwave at High
7 to 10 minutes, or until
noodles are tender.

Per Serving:
　Calories:　　111
　Sodium:　　274 mg.
　Cholesterol:　6 mg.
　Exchanges:　1 vegetable, 1½
　　　　　　　low fat meat

Easy Cream of ▲ Asparagus Soup

½ cup water
½ cup uncooked instant rice
¼ cup chopped onion
¼ cup chopped celery
1 pkg. (10 oz.) frozen
　asparagus cuts, defrosted
2 tablespoons flour
　Dash pepper
　Dash nutmeg
½ teaspoon salt, optional
1 teaspoon instant chicken
　bouillon granules
1½ cups skim milk
¼ teaspoon paprika

Serves 4

Microwave water in small bowl
at High 1½ to 2½ minutes, or
until boiling. Add rice. Let
stand, covered, 5 minutes, or
until water is absorbed. In 2-qt.
casserole combine onion, celery
and asparagus. Cover. Microwave at High 4 to 6 minutes, or
until tender, stirring twice.

Mash asparagus mixture with
fork. Stir in flour, seasonings,
rice and milk. Cover. Microwave
at High 7 to 8 minutes, or until
thickened. Sprinkle with paprika.

NOTE: for low sodium diet
substitute low-salt bouillon.

Per Serving:
　Calories:　　110
　Sodium:　　554 mg.
　Cholesterol:　0
　Exchanges:　½ milk, 1 vegetable,
　　　　　　　½ bread

Egg Drop Soup ►

4 cups hot water
2 teaspoons instant chicken
    bouillon granules
2 teaspoons soy sauce
1 green onion, chopped
2 eggs, slightly beaten

Serves 4

In 2-qt. casserole combine water, bouillon, soy sauce and onion. Microwave at High 7½ to 12 minutes, or until boiling. Pour eggs in a thin circular stream over boiling broth; let threads coagulate. Serve immediately.

NOTE: for low sodium diet substitute low-salt bouillon.

Per Serving:
Calories: 39
Sodium: 678 mg.
Cholesterol: 126 mg.
Exchanges: ½ med. fat meat

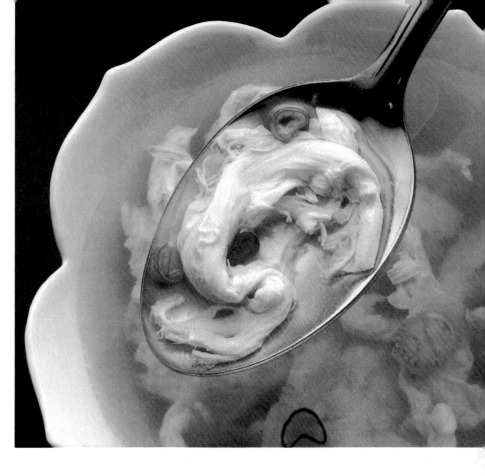

Cabbage Soup ►

2 slices bacon, chopped
6 cups chopped cabbage
1 medium onion, sliced and
    separated into rings
¼ teaspoon dill weed
¼ teaspoon caraway seed
⅛ teaspoon pepper
1½ teaspoons salt, optional
4 cups hot water, divided

Serves 6

Place bacon in 3-qt. casserole; cover. Microwave at High 3 to 5 minutes, or until bacon begins to crisp. Stir in cabbage, onion, seasonings and 2 cups water; cover. Microwave at High 10 minutes. Add remaining water; cover. Microwave at High 8 to 12 minutes, or until cabbage and onions are tender.

NOTE: for low sodium diet omit bacon.

Per Serving:
Calories: 48
Sodium: 547 mg.
Cholesterol: 12 mg.
Exchanges: 1 vegetable, ½ fat

French Onion Soup

2 tablespoons margarine or butter
1 large onion, sliced and separated into rings
3 cups hot water
3 teaspoons instant beef bouillon granules
½ teaspoon Worcestershire sauce
Dash pepper
2 slices thin bread, toasted
4 oz. shredded mozzarella cheese
4 teaspoons Parmesan cheese

Serves 4

Per Serving:
Calories:	135
Sodium:	158 mg.
Cholesterol:	15 mg.
Exchanges:	½ bread, ½ high fat meat, 1 fat

How to Microwave French Onion Soup

Combine margarine and onion in 2-qt. casserole. Cover. Microwave at High 8 to 11 minutes, or until onions are translucent and tender, stirring once or twice. Add water, bouillon, Worcestershire sauce and pepper. Re-cover.

Microwave at High 6 to 8 minutes, or until boiling. Reduce power to 50% (Medium). Microwave 5 minutes.

Divide soup into 4 individual casseroles or bowls. Top each with ½ slice toasted bread and 2 tablespoons mozzarella. Sprinkle with Parmesan. Place bowls in oven.

Microwave at High 2 to 3 minutes, or until cheese melts; rearrange bowls after half the time.

Spicy Tomato Soup ▲

2½ cups tomato juice or
    vegetable cocktail
2 teaspoons instant beef
    bouillon granules
1 teaspoon Worcestershire
    sauce
½ teaspoon basil
¼ teaspoon thyme
1 teaspoon parsley flakes
½ teaspoon sugar
4 lemon slices, optional

Serves 4

Combine all ingredients in
1-qt. casserole; cover. Microwave at High 1½ to 4 minutes,
or until heated. Pour into 4
serving bowls. Garnish each
with a lemon slice.

NOTE: for low sodium diet substitute low-salt bouillon and tomato
juice or vegetable cocktail.

Per Serving:
  Calories: 25
  Sodium: 700 mg.
  Cholesterol: 0
  Exchanges: 1 vegetable

Pumpkin Soup

5 green onions, chopped
2 tablespoons margarine or
    butter
1 can (16 oz.) pumpkin
¼ teaspoon ground ginger
⅛ teaspoon tumeric
1 cup evaporated skim milk
1 cup skim milk
2 cups hot water
2 teaspoons instant chicken
    bouillon granules
1 tablespoon sugar

Serves 4

Place onion and margarine in
3-qt. casserole. Microwave at
High 2½ to 3 minutes, or until
onion is tender, stirring once.
Blend in remaining ingredients.
Microwave at High 6 to 7
minutes, or until heated, stirring
every 2 minutes.

Per Serving:
  Calories: 181
  Sodium: 83 mg.
  Cholesterol: 0
  Exchanges: ½ skim milk, 1
                bread, 1½ fat

Split Pea Soup

4 cups hot water
1 cup green split peas
½ cup chopped onion
½ cup thinly sliced carrots
¼ cup thinly sliced celery
1 tablespoon parsley flakes
½ teaspoon marjoram leaves
½ teaspoon salt, optional
¼ teaspoon thyme leaves
⅛ teaspoon pepper

Serves 4

In 3-qt. casserole combine all
ingredients. Cover. Microwave
at High 8 to 10 minutes, or until
boiling. Stir. Reduce power to
50% (Medium). Microwave,
covered, 20 to 30 minutes, or
until peas are very soft. Remove
¾ to 1 cup peas. Mash
thoroughly and stir into soup.
Increase power to High. Microwave, uncovered, 10 to 15 minutes, or until slightly thickened.

Per Serving:
  Calories: 82
  Sodium: 275 mg.
  Cholesterol: 0
  Exchanges: ½ vegetable, 1
                bread

Sandwiches

When your diet is similar to what you're used to eating, you stay on it longer and feel less deprived. If you're used to having a sandwich for lunch, these recipes give you the type of food you like in a low calorie form. Add a soup or salad, but skip the potato chips.

◄ Mexican Pizza Sandwich

2 medium tomatoes, chopped
¼ cup chopped onion
1 tablespoon chopped green chili peppers
¼ teaspoon garlic powder
¼ teaspoon ground cumin
¼ teaspoon oregano leaves
¼ teaspoon basil leaves
Dash salt
Dash cayenne pepper
2 slices firm bread, toasted
2 tablespoons shredded mozzarella cheese

Serves 2

In 1-qt. casserole combine tomatoes, onion and chili peppers. Microwave at High 5 to 6 minutes, or until tomatoes are tender, stirring after half the time. Drain. Stir in seasonings.

Arrange toasted bread in bottom of 8 × 8-in. baking dish or on serving dish. Place half of tomato mixture on each slice. Top each with 1 tablespoon cheese. Microwave at High 1 to 2 minutes, or until cheese melts. Rotate sandwiches once during cooking.

Per Serving:
Calories: 134
Sodium: 150 mg.
Cholesterol: 9 mg.
Exchanges: 1 vegetable, 1
                 bread, ½ med.
                 fat meat

Zucchini Pocket Sandwich▲

1 cup shredded zucchini
½ cup sliced fresh mushrooms
1 cup chopped tomato
½ teaspoon basil leaves
¼ teaspoon garlic powder
2 tablespoons Parmesan
    cheese
4 small loaves pocket bread

Serves 4

In medium mixing bowl combine zucchini and mushrooms. Microwave at High 2 to 3 minutes, or until mushrooms are tender. Drain excess liquid.

Stir in tomato, seasonings and cheese. Split open one end of pocket bread. Place one-fourth of the filling in each.

Per Serving:
Calories: 114
Sodium: 140 mg.
Cholesterol: 8 mg.
Exchanges: 1 vegetable, 1
                 bread

Vegie Melt Sandwich

1 tablespoon low calorie
    mayonnaise*
½ teaspoon prepared mustard
2 slices firm bread, toasted
2 thin slices red onion
2 thin slices tomato
½ cup alfalfa sprouts
1 slice low fat American
    cheese, cut into 8 strips

Serves 2

In small bowl combine mayonnaise and mustard. Spread half of mixture on each slice of toast. Top each with 1 slice onion and tomato, then ¼ cup alfalfa sprouts. Arrange 4 strips cheese over each sandwich. Place on paper towel lined plate. Microwave at 50% (Medium) 1½ to 2½ minutes, or until cheese melts, rotating once during cooking.

*40 calories per tablespoon

Per Serving:
Calories: 118
Sodium: 280 mg.
Cholesterol: 3 mg.
Exchanges: 1 bread, ¼ low fat
                 meat, ½ fat

Cheesy Shrimp Sandwich

1 oz. Neufchâtel cheese
2 tablespoons chopped onion
2 tablespoons chopped celery
1 can (4¼ oz.) cooked shrimp,
    drained and rinsed
Dash celery seed
Dash salt, optional
Dash pepper
4 slices firm bread, toasted
16 thin slices cucumber

Serves 4

Place cheese, onion and celery in small mixing bowl or 1-qt. casserole. Microwave at 50% (Medium) 45 to 60 seconds, or until cheese softens. Add shrimp, celery seed, salt and pepper.

Place 4 cucumber slices on each slice of toast. Top each with one-fourth of shrimp mixture.

Per Serving:
Calories: 100
Sodium: 80 mg.
Cholesterol: 27 mg.
Exchanges: ½ bread, 1 low fat
                 meat

Beverages

When you feel tired or hungry, a hot beverage can refresh you and quiet hunger. It helps you feel full without adding a lot of calories. Begin a meal slowly by sipping a hot beverage, and you'll feel satisfied with less food.

◄ Spiced Coffee

4 cups hot water
1 stick cinnamon
1 teaspoon whole allspice
1 tablespoon sugar
  Dash nutmeg
1 tablespoon instant coffee
  Lemon twists or cinnamon
  sticks, optional

Serves 4
Serving size: 1 cup

Combine water, 1 stick cinnamon, allspice, sugar and nutmeg in 1-qt. mixing bowl. Microwave at High 6 to 8 minutes, or until mixture comes to a full, rolling boil. Immediately remove from oven; strain. Pour mixture over instant coffee in a serving pot. Stir to dissolve.

If desired, serve with a twist of lemon or a cinnamon stick.

Per Serving:
Calories: 8
Sodium: 0
Cholesterol: 0
Exchanges: free

Café au lait

2 cups skim milk
2 cups water
1½ tablespoons instant coffee
4 tablespoons non-dairy
  frozen whipped topping,
  optional
  Dash nutmeg

Serves 4
Serving size: 1 cup

In 2-qt. casserole combine milk and water. Cover. Microwave at High 5 to 8 minutes, or until hot but not boiling. Blend in coffee until dissolved. Pour into 4 cups. Garnish with whipped topping, if desired. Sprinkle each serving with nutmeg.

Per Serving:
Calories: 50
Sodium: 78 mg.
Cholesterol: 4 mg.
Exchanges: ½ milk

Hot Chocolate

3 tablespoons unsweetened
  cocoa
2 tablespoons fructose
3 cups skim milk
1 teaspoon vanilla
1 cup water

Serves 4
Serving size: 1 cup

Combine cocoa and fructose in small dish. Set aside. Place remaining ingredients in 2-qt. casserole. Stir in cocoa mixture and beat with a wire whip. Cover. Microwave at High 6 to 8 minutes, or until hot but not boiling, beating with wire whip halfway through cooking.

Per Serving:
Calories: 94
Sodium: 174 mg.
Cholesterol: 5 mg.
Exchanges: 1 milk, ½ fruit

Spiced Tomato Cocktail ▲

1 cup water
1 teaspoon instant beef
   bouillon granules
   Dash cayenne pepper
½ teaspoon summer savory
2 cups tomato juice
   Dash garlic powder
   Celery stalk or green onion

Serves 6
Serving size: ½ cup

Combine all ingredients except celery in 2-qt. casserole. Cover. Microwave at High 5 to 10 minutes, or until boiling. Garnish with celery or green onion.

NOTE: for low sodium diet substitute low-salt bouillon and tomato juice.

Per Serving:
   Calories: 16
   Sodium: 481 mg.
   Cholesterol: 0
   Exchanges: ½ vegetable

Hot Bouillon

1 cup water
1 teaspoon instant beef
   bouillon granules
1 stalk celery

Serves 1

Place water in coffee mug. Microwave at High 1 to 2½ minutes, or until boiling. Stir in bouillon until dissolved. Serve hot, garnished with celery stalk.

NOTE: for low sodium diet substitute low-salt bouillon.

Per Serving:
   Calories: 25
   Sodium: 943 mg.
   Cholesterol: 0
   Exchanges: 1 vegetable

Fresh Cranberry Juice ▲

1 lb. cranberries
6 cups hot water
¼ cup fructose

Serves 12
Serving size: ½ cup

In 5-qt. casserole combine cranberries and water. Cover. Microwave at High 20 to 25 minutes, or until cranberries split. Strain. Stir in fructose and chill. Serve mixed with orange juice or use in recipes on following page.

Per Serving:
   Calories: 27
   Sodium: 0
   Cholesterol: 0
   Exchanges: ¾ fruit

Hot Mulled Cider ▲

½ teaspoon whole allspice
½ teaspoon whole cloves
1 stick cinnamon
½ cup water
1½ cups Fresh Cranberry
    Juice, opposite
1 qt. apple cider

Serves 12
Serving size: ½ cup

In 2-qt. casserole combine all ingredients. Cover. Microwave at High 5 to 8 minutes, or until hot. Strain to remove spices.

Per Serving:
Calories: 45
Sodium: 0
Cholesterol: 0
Exchanges: 1 fruit

Spiced Tea

4 cups hot water
1 tablespoon grated orange
    peel
1 teaspoon grated lemon peel
6 whole cloves
1 stick cinnamon
3 tea bags

Serves 4
Serving size: 1 cup

In 2-qt. casserole combine water, orange peel, lemon peel and spices. Cover. Microwave at High 6 to 10 minutes, or until boiling. Remove from oven; immediately add tea bags and let steep 3 to 5 minutes. Serve hot or chilled.

Per Serving:
Calories: 0
Sodium: 0
Cholesterol: 0
Exchanges: free

Citrus Warmer ▲

2 cups unsweetened orange
    juice
1 cup water
1 cup Fresh Cranberry Juice,
    opposite
½ cup pineapple juice
1 tablespoon lemon juice
2 drops red food coloring,
    optional
Mint leaves

Serves 8
Serving size: ½ cup

In 2-qt. casserole combine the liquids; cover. Microwave at High 10 to 12 minutes, or until boiling. Reduce power to 50% (Medium). Simmer 5 minutes. Serve hot, garnished with mint.

Per Serving:
Calories: 24
Sodium: 0
Cholesterol: 0
Exchanges: 1½ fruit

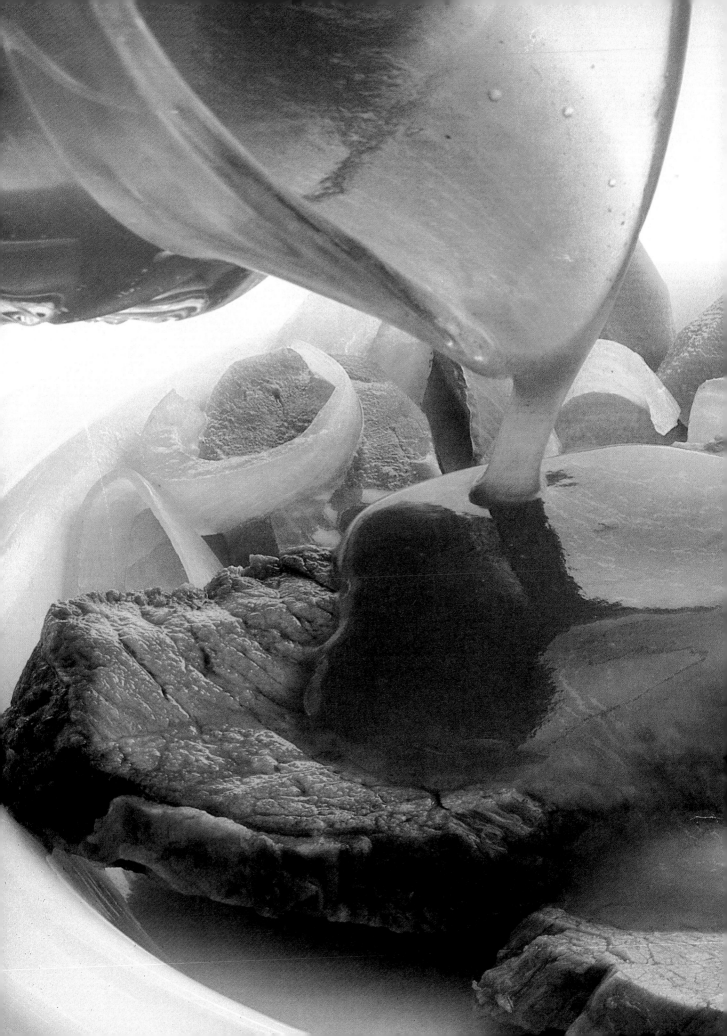

Meats

These recipes provide a variety of meat dishes, high in protein and trimmed of excess calories. It is important to use lean meat and to trim all visible fat before microwaving. The portions here may be smaller than you are used to eating, but they are nutritionally adequate. Fad diets featuring all the steak you can eat are usually too high in both calories and protein for the average person. Excess calories, even from protein, are converted by the body to fat.

◄ Stuffed Flank Steak

1 pkg. (10 oz.) frozen
   asparagus spears
1 tablespoon steak sauce
1 tablespoon water
1½ lbs. flank steak, pounded
   to ¼-in. thickness
¼ teaspoon pepper

Serves 6

Microwave asparagus package at High 3 to 5 minutes, or until it flexes easily. Drain. Combine steak sauce and water. Brush steak with half of mixture. Place asparagus on steak. Sprinkle with pepper. Roll steak jelly-roll style. Place in 8 × 8-in. baking dish. Brush with remaining mixture. Cover with wax paper. Microwave at High 5 minutes. Reduce power to 50% (Medium). Microwave 15 to 20 minutes, or until internal temperature is 150°; rotate dish once.

Per Serving:
  Calories: 186
  Sodium: 102 mg.
  Cholesterol: 77 mg.
  Exchanges: 1 vegetable, 3 low
                   fat meat

Roast Tenderloin ▲

¼ teaspoon garlic powder
¼ teaspoon onion powder
2 lb. beef tenderloin roast

Serves 8

Combine garlic and onion powders. Rub well over surface of roast. Place tenderloin on roasting rack in 12 × 8-in. baking dish. Shield ends and 1 inch down sides of tenderloin with aluminum foil. Microwave at High 3 minutes. Reduce power to 50% (Medium). Microwave 5 minutes. Turn roast over and rotate dish; remove shielding. Microwave at 50% (Medium) 8 to 12 minutes longer, or until internal temperature reaches 125°. (Roast will be medium rare). Let stand, tented loosely with foil, 10 minutes. Temperature will rise 15° to 20°.

Per Serving:
  Calories: 165
  Sodium: 94 mg.
  Cholesterol: 77 mg.
  Exchanges: 3 low fat meat

Sauerbraten

1 cup wine vinegar
1¼ cups water, divided
½ teaspoon salt, optional
5 peppercorns
⅛ teaspoon ground cloves
⅝ teaspoon ginger, divided
3 bay leaves
1 clove garlic, crushed
2 teaspoons caraway seeds
1½ to 2 lbs. top round steak,
    1½ to 2-in. thick
2 small onions, thinly sliced
2 medium carrots, sliced
1 tablespoon cornstarch
¼ teaspoon bouquet sauce

Serves 8

Per Serving:	
Calories:	179
Sodium:	214 mg.
Cholesterol:	77 mg.
Exchanges:	½ vegetable,
	3 low fat meat

How to Microwave Sauerbraten

Combine vinegar, 1 cup water, salt, peppercorns, cloves, ⅛ teaspoon ginger, bay leaves, garlic and caraway in small mixing bowl to make marinade. Microwave at High 3 minutes.

Place meat in large plastic bag. Pour in marinade. Refrigerate 2 to 3 days. Strain marinade, discarding all but ½ cup.

Arrange meat, onions, carrots and ½ cup marinade in 2-qt. casserole. Cover. Microwave at High 3 minutes. Reduce power to 50% (Medium).

Microwave 45 to 75 minutes, or until meat is fork tender, turning over after half the time. Remove meat and vegetables and set on covered platter.

Remove 1 cup broth from casserole; discard remainder. In casserole blend cornstarch, ¼ cup water, ½ teaspoon ginger and bouquet sauce. Add broth.

Increase power to High. Microwave 4 to 6 minutes, or until thickened, stirring 2 or 3 times. Slice roast thinly and pour sauce over slices.

45

◄ Ginger Beef

2 tablespoons water
2 tablespoons soy sauce
¼ teaspoon bouquet sauce,
  optional
1 tablespoon cornstarch
¼ teaspoon ginger
⅛ teaspoon garlic powder
1 lb. flank steak, thinly sliced
1 medium green pepper,
  cut into thin strips
4 small green onions, chopped
1 tomato, cut into wedges

Serves 6

In 2-qt. casserole blend water,
soy sauce, bouquet sauce,
cornstarch, ginger and garlic
powder. Add flank steak, stirring
to coat. Stir in green pepper
and onion. Microwave at High 8
to 10 minutes, or until meat and
green pepper are tender,
stirring 2 or 3 times. Stir in
tomatoes. Microwave at High 1
to 2 minutes, or until tomatoes
are heated through.

NOTE: if desired, serve over
rice. See Exchange Chart,
page 10.

Per Serving:
  Calories: 122
  Sodium: 178 mg.
  Cholesterol: 51 mg.
  Exchanges: ½ vegetable, 2 low
                   fat meat

Beef Burgundy ▲

¼ cup water
¼ cup burgundy wine
1 tablespoon cornstarch
1 lb. boneless sirloin, cut
  into ¾-in. cubes
1 small onion, chopped
8 oz. sliced fresh mushrooms
½ teaspoon salt, optional
¼ teaspoon garlic powder
¼ teaspoon pepper

Serves 4

Blend water, wine and
cornstarch in 3-qt. casserole.
Stir in remaining ingredients;
cover. Microwave at High 3
minutes. Reduce power to 50%
(Medium). Microwave 20 to 30
minutes, or until meat is fork
tender, stirring once or twice.
Let stand, covered, 5 minutes.

NOTE: if desired, serve over
rice. See Exchange Chart,
page 10.

Per Serving:
  Calories: 198
  Sodium: 322 mg.
  Cholesterol: 77 mg.
  Exchanges: 1 vegetable,
                   3 low fat meat

Cube Steak With ▲ Fresh Vegetables

4 cube steaks
1 medium onion, cut into 8 wedges
1 medium zucchini, cut into ¼-in. slices
1 medium tomato, cut into wedges
2 tablespoons white wine
½ teaspoon dill

Serves 4

Place steaks on roasting rack. Microwave at High 6 to 8 minutes, or until meat is no longer pink, rearranging after half the cooking time. Drain and set aside.

In medium mixing bowl combine onion, zucchini, tomatoes, wine and dill. Cover with plastic wrap. Microwave at High 6 to 9 minutes, or until onions are translucent and zucchini is tender, stirring two or three times during cooking. Place mixture on steaks. Microwave 2 to 3 minutes, or until tomato and steaks are heated thoroughly.

Per Serving:
Calories: 187
Sodium: 69 mg.
Cholesterol: 77 mg.
Exchanges: 1 vegetable, 3 low fat meat

Flank & Tomato Curry ▶

1 to 1½ lbs. flank steak, thinly sliced
¼ cup thinly sliced celery
¼ cup chopped onion
¼ cup chopped green pepper
1 tablespoon cornstarch
1 can (16 oz.) whole tomatoes, drained, juice reserved
1 teaspoon curry
1 teaspoon salt, optional
¼ teaspoon pepper

Serves 6

In 2-qt. casserole combine flank steak, celery, onion and green pepper. Microwave at High 7 to 11 minutes, or until meat is no longer pink and vegetables are tender, stirring 2 or 3 times during cooking.

Blend cornstarch into reserved tomato juice. Add cornstarch mixture, tomatoes, curry, salt and pepper to meat mixture. Stir to break apart tomatoes. Microwave at High 7 to 12 minutes, or until meat is tender and flavors blended.

NOTE: if desired, serve over rice. See Exchange Chart, page 10.

Per Serving:
Calories: 194
Sodium: 282 mg.
Cholesterol: 118 mg.
Exchanges: 1 vegetable, 3 low fat meat

◄Beef Stew

1 lb. chuck stew meat
1 medium potato, cut into
　½-in. chunks
1 medium onion, cut into
　eighths
3 medium stalks celery, sliced
3 medium carrots, sliced
½ teaspoon basil
½ teaspoon salt, optional
¼ teaspoon pepper
½ teaspoon marjoram
2 medium tomatoes, chopped
1 can (12 oz.) light beer
¼ cup water
1 tablespoon cornstarch

Serves 6

In 3-qt. casserole combine all
ingredients except water and
cornstarch. In 1-cup measure
blend water and cornstarch; stir
into casserole. Cover. Microwave at High 10 minutes. Reduce power to 50% (Medium).
Microwave 45 to 60 minutes, or
until meat is fork tender, stirring
once or twice. Let stand,
covered, 5 to 10 minutes.

Per Serving:
　Calories:　　　160
　Sodium:　　　244 mg.
　Cholesterol:　52 mg.
　Exchanges:　　1½ vegetable, 2
　　　　　　　　　low fat meat

Chili With Round Steak ▲

1½ lbs. round steak, cut into
　¾-in. cubes
1 medium green pepper,
　chopped
1 medium onion, chopped
1 clove garlic, minced
2 to 3 teaspoons chili
　powder
1 teaspoon cumin
2 cans (16 oz. each) whole
　tomatoes, undrained
1 can (15½ oz.) kidney
　beans, drained and
　rinsed

Serves 4

In 3-qt. casserole combine all
ingredients; cover. Microwave at
High 5 minutes. Remove　.
cover. Stir to break apart
tomatoes. Reduce power to
50% (Medium). Microwave,
uncovered, 40 to 60 minutes, or
until meat is fork tender, stirring
2 or 3 times. Let stand,
covered, 10 minutes.

Per Serving:
　Calories:　　　380
　Sodium:　　　231 mg.
　Cholesterol:　115 mg.
　Exchanges:　　2½ vegetable, 1
　　　　　　　　　bread, 4½ meat

Burgers With Mushroom Sauce

1 lb. extra lean ground beef
1 small onion, chopped
1 tablespoon dry vegetable flakes
1 teaspoon Worcestershire sauce
½ teaspoon salt, optional
¼ teaspoon pepper
1 teaspoon prepared horseradish
8 oz. sliced fresh mushrooms
1 teaspoon soy sauce
¼ teaspoon dry mustard
¼ cup white wine
1 tablespoon cornstarch
¼ cup water

Serves 4

In medium mixing bowl combine ground beef, onion, vegetable flakes, Worcestershire sauce, salt, pepper and horseradish. Form into 4 patties. Place in 12 × 8-in. baking dish.

Microwave at High 5 to 9 minutes, or until meat is no longer pink, rearranging after half the cooking time. Remove patties and set aside, reserving meat juices.

Add remaining ingredients to meat juices. Microwave at High 6 to 9 minutes, or until sauce is thickened and mushrooms are tender, stirring 2 or 3 times. Return patties to dish. Microwave at High 1 to 2 minutes, or until heated through.

NOTE: for low sodium diet substitute low-salt soy sauce.

Per Serving:
Calories: 198
Sodium: 425 mg.
Cholesterol: 77 mg.
Exchanges: 1 vegetable, 3 low fat meat

Florentine Stuffed Meatloaf ▲

1 lb. extra lean ground beef
1 egg, slightly beaten
1 small onion, chopped
¼ teaspoon salt, optional
¼ teaspoon pepper

2 pkgs. (10 oz. each) frozen chopped spinach
½ teaspoon nutmeg
½ cup shredded mozzarella cheese

Serves 4

Combine meat, egg, onion, salt and pepper. Line sides and bottom of 9 × 5-in. loaf dish with two-thirds of meat mixture. Set aside.

Place spinach packages in oven. Microwave at High 4 to 6 minutes, or until warm. Drain spinach thoroughly.

In medium bowl, combine spinach and nutmeg. Spread half of spinach over meat in pan. Press slightly. Sprinkle cheese over spinach. Top with remaining spinach; press lightly. Form remaining meat over top, sealing seams. Microwave at High 10 to 15 minutes, or until top of loaf is no longer pink and internal temperature is 150°. Let stand 3 to 5 minutes.

Per Serving:
Calories: 290   Cholesterol: 147 mg.
Sodium: 188 mg. Exchanges: 2 vegetable, 4 low fat meat, ½ fat

Stuffed Peppers

1 lb. extra lean ground beef
1 small onion, chopped
1 medium tomato, chopped
1 cup cooked rice
1 teaspoon prepared
  horseradish
4 large green peppers, seeds
  and pulp removed
1 slice low fat cheese, cut into
  8 thin strips

Serves 4

In medium mixing bowl combine crumbled ground beef, onion, tomato, rice and horseradish. Mix well. Fill green peppers with meat mixture.

Place a few wooden picks around bottom of peppers to hold up if needed.

Place on roasting rack. Cover with wax paper. Microwave at High 13 to 17 minutes, or until meat is no longer pink and peppers are tender, rearranging after half the cooking time. Top each pepper with 2 strips of cheese. Microwave 1 to 2 minutes, or until cheese melts.

Per Serving
Calories: 246
Sodium: 137 mg.
Cholesterol: 79 mg.
Exchanges: 1½ vegetable,
                   ½ bread, 3 low
                   fat meat

Cabbage Rolls

8 medium cabbage leaves

Filling:

1 lb. extra lean ground beef
1 egg
¼ cup chopped onion
¼ cup chopped green pepper
1 teaspoon Worcestershire
  sauce
⅛ teaspoon garlic powder
1 teaspoon prepared hot
  mustard
¼ teaspoon salt, optional
⅛ teaspoon pepper
1 teaspoon prepared
  horseradish

Sauce:

1 cup tomato juice
½ teaspoon basil leaves
½ teaspoon oregano leaves

Serves 4

Microwave whole cabbage at High 2 minutes, or until 8 outer leaves can be separated easily. Remove stem end of each leaf by cutting a 'V'. Arrange leaves in 12 × 8-in. baking dish. Cover with plastic wrap. Microwave at High 2 to 4 minutes, or until leaves are tender and pliable.

In medium bowl blend all filling ingredients. Place one-eighth of the meat mixture on base of each leaf. Fold in sides of leaf; roll up. Place seam side down in 12 × 8-in. baking dish.

Combine sauce ingredients. Pour over rolls; cover. Microwave at High 7 to 12 minutes, or until centers of rolls are no longer pink, rearranging rolls after half the cooking time.

NOTE: for low sodium diet substitute low-salt tomato juice.

Per Serving:
Calories: 190
Sodium: 359 mg.
Cholesterol: 110 mg.
Exchanges: ½ vegetable, 3
                   low fat meat, ½ fat

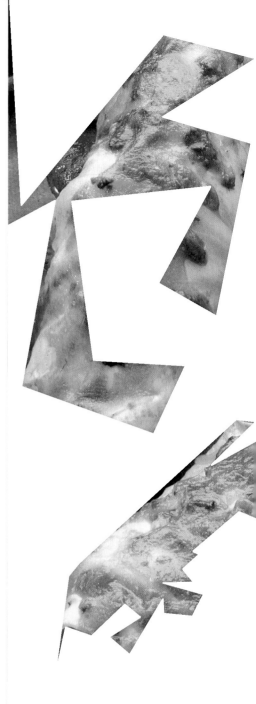

Meatballs With Tomato &▲ Green Pepper Sauce

Tomato & Green Pepper
Sauce, page 129
1 lb. extra lean ground beef
1 egg
½ cup grated carrot
½ teaspoon salt, optional
¼ teaspoon pepper

Serves 4

Prepare Tomato & Green
Pepper Sauce as directed. Set
aside. Blend remaining ingredients. Form into 12 meatballs.
Arrange in 12 × 8-in. baking
dish. Cover with wax paper.
Microwave at High 6 to 9
minutes, or until meatballs are
firm and no longer pink,
rearranging after half the
cooking time. Drain; set aside.

Microwave sauce at High 1 to 3
minutes, or until heated through.
Serve over meatballs.

Per Serving:
Calories: 237
Sodium: 590 mg.
Cholesterol: 140 mg.
Exchanges: 2 vegetable, 3 low
              fat meat, ½ fat

Taco Dinner Salad

1 lb. extra lean ground beef
1 medium onion, chopped
¼ cup catsup
2 teaspoons chili powder
1 teaspoon ground cumin
½ teaspoon salt, optional
¼ teaspoon pepper
6 cups shredded lettuce
2 large tomatoes, chopped

Serves 4

In 1-qt. casserole combine
crumbled ground beef and
onion. Microwave at High 4 to 8
minutes, or until beef is no
longer pink, stirring once or
twice. Drain well. Stir in catsup,
chili powder, cumin, salt and
pepper. Microwave at High 1½
to 3½ minutes, or until very hot,
stirring once or twice.

Divide lettuce and tomatoes into
4 serving bowls. Add one-fourth
ground beef mixture to each
bowl; toss if desired.

NOTE: for low sodium diet
substitute low-salt catsup.

Per Serving:
Calories: 195
Sodium: 504 mg.
Cholesterol: 77 mg.
Exchanges: 1½ vegetable,
              3 low fat meat

Spaghetti Sauce ▶

1 lb. extra lean ground beef
1 small onion, chopped
1 can (6 oz.) tomato paste
1 can (16 oz.) whole tomatoes
2 tablespoons grated
·   Parmesan cheese
½ cup water
1 teaspoon oregano leaves
1 teaspoon basil leaves
½ teaspoon salt, optional
¼ teaspoon pepper
⅛ teaspoon ground sage

Serves 4

In 2-qt. casserole combine
crumbled ground beef and
onion. Microwave at High 4 to 6
minutes, or until meat is no
longer pink, stirring after half the
time. Stir in remaining
ingredients. Microwave at High
5 minutes. Reduce power to
50% (Medium). Microwave 15 to
20 minutes, or until sauce
thickens and flavors blend,
stirring 2 or 3 times.

Per Serving:
Calories: 248
Sodium: 550 mg.
Cholesterol: 85 mg.
Exchanges: 3 vegetable,
              1 bread, 3 low
              fat meat, ½ fat

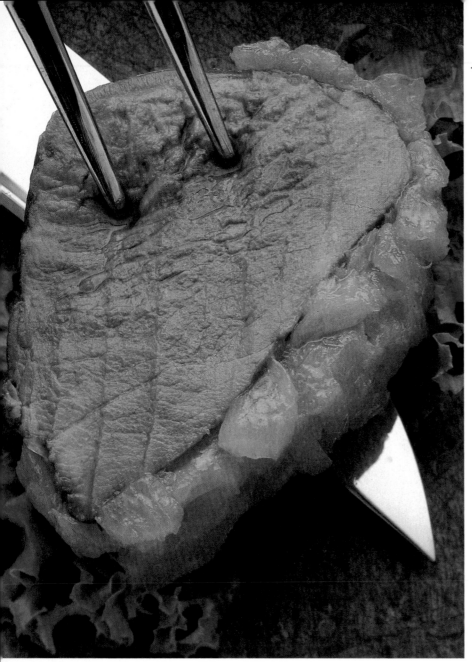

Pineapple Glaze

1 can (8 oz.) crushed
    pineapple, drained
1 teaspoon prepared mustard
⅛ to ¼ teaspoon thyme leaves
1 teaspoon brown sugar

Makes 1 cup
Serving size: 2 tablespoons

Combine ingredients in small
bowl or 2-cup measure. Microwave at High 1 to 2 minutes, or
until heated. Spread over pork
tenderloin roast as directed.

Per Serving:
  Calories: 17
  Sodium: 0
  Cholesterol: 0
  Exchanges: ½ fruit

Fruit Glaze

½ cup low sugar apple or
    cherry spread

Makes ½ cup
Serving size: 1 tablespoon

Spread fruit over pork tenderloin
roast as directed.

Per Serving:
  Calories: 12
  Sodium: 0
  Cholesterol: 0
  Exchanges: free

Apple Glaze

½ cup unsweetened
    applesauce
¼ teaspoon nutmeg

Makes ½ cup
Serving size: 1 tablespoon

Mix applesauce and nutmeg.
Spread on pork tenderloin roast
as directed.

Per Serving:
  Calories: 5
  Sodium: 0
  Cholesterol: 0
  Exchanges: free

Pork Tenderloin

2 lb. pork tenderloin roast

Serves 8

Cooking time: 12½ to 16½ minutes per lb.

Place tenderloin on roasting rack in 12 × 8-in. baking dish. Shield
ends of roast with aluminum foil. Estimate total cooking time; divide
in half. Microwave at High 3 minutes. Reduce power to 50%
(Medium). Microwave remaining part of first half of time. Remove
foil. Turn roast over. Spread one of the following fruit glazes over
roast, if desired. Microwave at 50% (Medium) the remaining time,
or until the internal temperature reaches 165°. Tent loosely with foil.
Let stand 5 to 10 minutes, or until temperature is 170°.

Per Serving:
  Calories: 256   Cholesterol: 75 mg.
  Sodium: 69 mg. Exchanges: 3 med. fat meat

Basic Pork Chops

1½ teaspoons bouquet sauce
2 teaspoons water
4 lean pork chops, ½-in. thick

Serves 4

Cooking Time: 16½ to 18½ minutes per lb.

In small dish, combine bouquet sauce and water. Place pork chops on roasting rack; brush with half of bouquet sauce mixture. Cover with wax paper. Estimate total cooking time. Microwave at 50% (Medium) for half the total cooking time. Turn over and rearrange chops. Brush with remaining bouquet mixture. Microwave at 50% (Medium) for remaining time, or until meat is no longer pink.

Per Serving:
Calories: 234
Sodium: 173 mg.
Cholesterol: 76 mg.
Exchanges: 3 med. fat meat

Pork Chop Bake ▶

4 lean pork chops, ½-in. thick
4 thin onion slices
4 green pepper rings
1 medium tomato, sliced
2 tablespoons Parmesan cheese

Serves 4

Preheat 10-in. browning dish at High 5 minutes. Place pork chops on dish. When sizzling stops, turn chops over and top with onion and green pepper. Reduce power to 50% (Medium). Microwave 7 to 10 minutes, or until meat is no longer pink; rearrange chops after half the time. Top each chop with tomato slice and Parmesan cheese during last 2 minutes.

Per Serving:
Calories: 262
Sodium: 57 mg.
Cholesterol: 84 mg.
Exchanges: 1 vegetable, 3 med. fat meat

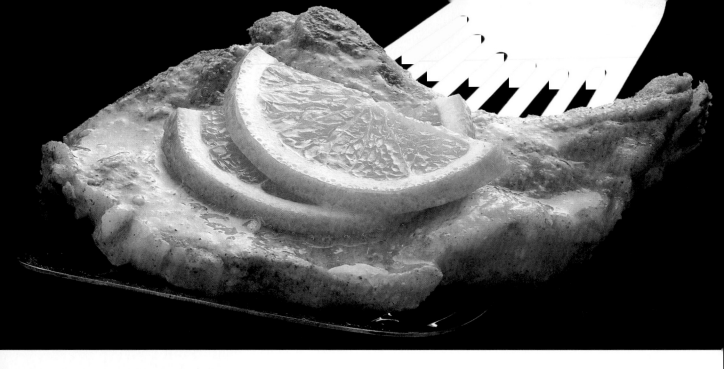

◄Bavarian Pork Chops

1 can (16 oz.) sauerkraut, drained
1 teaspoon vinegar
1 teaspoon sugar
¼ teaspoon cinnamon
   Dash nutmeg
   Dash salt, optional
   Dash pepper
¼ teaspoon caraway seed
1 medium apple, diced
4 lean pork chops, ½-in. thick
2 teaspoons Worcestershire sauce

Serves 4

In 8 × 8-in. baking dish, combine sauerkraut, vinegar, sugar, cinnamon, nutmeg, salt, pepper, caraway and apple. Top with pork chops. Brush each chop with Worcestershire sauce. Cover with waxed paper.

Microwave at High 5 minutes. Rearrange chops; reduce power to 50% (Medium). Microwave 7 to 15 minutes, or until meat near bone is no longer pink.

Per Serving:
Calories: 274
Sodium: 268 mg.
Cholesterol: 76 mg.
Exchanges: 1 vegetable, ½ fruit, 3 med. fat meat

Pork Chops With▲ Citrus Sauce

4 lean pork chops, ½-in. thick
¼ cup orange juice
1 teaspoon lemon juice
   Dash ground ginger
   Dash salt, optional
   Dash pepper
¼ teaspoon cinnamon
1 small orange, sliced

Serves 4

Arrange chops in 8 × 8-in. baking dish, with meatiest portions to outside of dish. In small bowl or 1-cup measure combine juices and seasonings. Pour over chops. Cover with wax paper. Microwave at High 5 minutes.

Turn over and rearrange chops. Reduce power to 50% (Medium). Microwave 7 to 14 minutes, or until meat near bone is no longer pink. Garnish each chop with orange slice.

Per Serving:
Calories: 249
Sodium: 23 mg.
Cholesterol: 76 mg.
Exchanges: ½ fruit, 3 med. fat meat

Pork Stew

1 cup hot water
1 teaspoon instant chicken
    bouillon granules
¼ teaspoon bouquet sauce
2 tablespoons all-purpose
    flour
1 lb. lean boneless pork,
    cut into 1-in. cubes
1 large onion, thinly sliced
1 cup thinly sliced celery
1 can (16 oz.) whole tomatoes
8 oz. green beans, cut into
    1-in. lengths
2 medium yellow squash,
    thinly sliced
½ teaspoon crushed rosemary
¼ teaspoon salt, optional
    Dash pepper
⅛ teaspoon garlic powder
2 cups shredded lettuce

Serves 6

In 2-cup measure, blend hot water, bouillon, bouquet sauce and flour. Set aside.

Place remaining ingredients except lettuce in 3-qt. casserole. Stir in flour and water mixture. Cover. Microwave at High 10 minutes. Stir. Re-cover.

Reduce power to 50% (Medium). Microwave 35 to 40 minutes, or until meat and vegetables are tender. Stir in lettuce. Let stand, covered, 5 to 10 minutes.

NOTE: for low sodium diet substitute low-salt bouillon and bouquet sauce.

Per Serving:
Calories: 240
Sodium: 304 mg.
Cholesterol: 49 mg.
Exchanges: 1 vegetable, 1
    bread, 2 med.
    fat meat

Oriental Pork Rolls ▶

¾ lb. lean boneless pork
    tenderloin, cubed
4 green onions, sliced
8 oz. fresh sliced mushrooms
4 oz. fresh bean sprouts
2 tablespoons chopped sweet
    red pepper
1 can (8 oz.) water chestnuts,
    sliced
1 tablespoon soy sauce
1 teaspoon instant beef
    bouillon granules
4 to 6 lettuce leaves
½ to ¾ cup cold water
1 tablespoon cornstarch

Serves 4

NOTE: for low sodium diet
substitute low-salt soy sauce
and bouillon.

Per Serving:
   Calories: 202
   Sodium: 327 mg.
   Cholesterol: 49 mg.
   Exchanges: 1½ vegetable, 2
                   med. fat meat

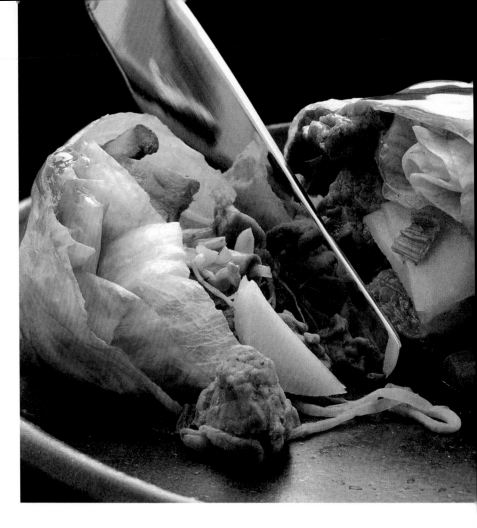

How to Microwave Oriental Pork Rolls

Combine pork and onions in 2-qt. casserole; cover. Microwave at High 5 to 7 minutes, or until meat is no longer pink, stirring after half the cooking time. Drain.

Mix in mushrooms, sprouts, red pepper, water chestnuts, soy sauce and bouillon. Cover. Microwave at High 6 to 8 minutes, or until tender, stirring twice. Drain, reserving liquid.

Place lettuce head in 2-qt. casserole; cover. Microwave at High 30 to 60 seconds, or until outer leaves are pliable. Remove 4 to 6 leaves. Refrigerate remainder for future use.

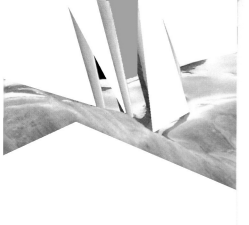

Pork & Pepper With Pineapple Rice

¼ cup hot water
1 can (8 oz.) crushed
   pineapple, undrained
⅔ cup instant rice
¾ lb. lean boneless pork, cut
   into thin strips
1 medium green pepper, cut
   into thin strips

⅓ cup cold water
1 tablespoon soy sauce
2 teaspoons cornstarch
1 teaspoon grated orange rind
¼ teaspoon black pepper

Serves 4

Place hot water and pineapple in 1-qt. casserole. Microwave at High 1½ to 3 minutes, or until boiling. Stir in rice; cover. Set aside.

In 1½-qt. casserole combine pork and pepper strips; cover. Microwave at High 4 to 5 minutes, or until meat is no longer pink, stirring once. Drain.

In 1-cup measure combine cold water, soy sauce, cornstarch, orange rind and black pepper. Pour over meat and pepper strips.

Microwave at High 1 to 3 minutes, or until sauce is thickened and pork is tender. Serve over pineapple rice. If necessary, microwave rice at High 1 to 2 minutes, to reheat.

Per Serving:
  Calories: 235   Cholesterol: 50 mg.
  Sodium: 138 mg.   Exchanges: ½ fruit, 1 bread, 2 med. fat meat

Spoon 2 to 4 tablespoons meat mixture on each softened lettuce leaf. Fold up leaf to enclose filling.

Arrange seam side down in 12 × 8-in. baking dish. Cover with plastic wrap. Microwave at High 4 to 6 minutes, or until heated through. Set aside and keep warm.

Add water to reserved liquid to make 1 cup. Blend in cornstarch. Microwave at High 3 to 5 minutes, or until thickened and bubbly, stirring twice. Serve over rolls.

Veal With Vegetables

1 lb. boneless veal, pounded
    to ¼-in. thickness, cut
    into serving pieces
1 medium onion, thinly sliced
    and separated into rings
1 can (6 oz.) tomato paste
1 tablespoon all-purpose flour
½ teaspoon basil leaves
½ teaspoon oregano leaves
2 teaspoons parsley flakes
¼ teaspoon garlic powder
¼ teaspoon salt, optional
¼ teaspoon black pepper
2 large tomatoes, peeled
    and chopped
1 cup thinly sliced zucchini
1 medium green pepper, cut
    into thin strips

Serves 4

Pound veal well with mallet or saucer edge to flatten and tenderize.

Place veal in 12 × 8-in. baking dish. Top with onion rings. In medium bowl blend tomato paste, flour, basil, oregano, parsley, garlic powder, salt and pepper. Stir in tomatoes, zucchini and green pepper. Spread vegetable mixture over veal. Cover with wax paper. Microwave at High 13 to 18 minutes, or until veal is no longer pink and vegetables are tender, rearranging veal after 8 minutes cooking time.

Per Serving:
  Calories: 231
  Sodium: 210 mg.
  Cholesterol: 86 mg.
  Exchanges: 2½ vegetable, 4
                    low fat meat

Mushroom Veal

1 lb. boneless veal, pounded to
⅟₄-in. thickness, cut into
serving pieces
8 oz. sliced fresh mushrooms
⅓ cup water
2 tablespoons white wine
2 teaspoons all-purpose flour

2 teaspoons dried chives
2 teaspoons lemon juice
½ teaspoon instant beef
bouillon granules
⅛ teaspoon salt, optional
⅛ teaspoon bouquet sauce,
optional

Serves 4

Arrange veal in 12 × 8-in. baking dish. Top with sliced mushrooms.
Cover with wax paper. Microwave at 50% (Medium) 7 to 10
minutes, or until veal is tender and no longer pink; rearrange veal
once, leaving mushrooms on top. Set aside.

In small bowl blend remaining ingredients. Increase power to High.
Microwave 1½ to 4 minutes, or until thickened, stirring with wire
whip once or twice. Pour sauce over veal; cover with wax paper.

Reduce power to 50% (Medium). Microwave 1½ to 3½ minutes, or
until heated through.

Per Serving:
Calories: 180   Cholesterol: 86 mg.
Sodium: 262 mg.   Exchanges: ½ vegetable, 3 low fat meat

Veal Mozzarella

1 can (8 oz.) tomato paste
¼ teaspoon oregano leaves
½ teaspoon basil leaves
¼ teaspoon garlic powder
¼ teaspoon salt, optional
¼ teaspoon sugar
⅛ teaspoon pepper

1 lb. boneless veal, pounded
to ¼-in. thickness, cut into
serving pieces
¾ cup shredded mozzarella
cheese
1 tablespoon parsley flakes

Serves 4

Combine all ingredients except veal, cheese and parsley in small
bowl. Microwave at High 2 minutes. Reduce power to 50%
(Medium). Microwave 6 minutes. Set aside.

Place veal in 12 × 8-in. baking dish. Cover with wax paper.
Microwave at 50% (Medium) 6 to 9 minutes, or until veal is no
longer pink, rearranging once. Drain. Cover with sauce. Sprinkle
cheese and parsley on top; cover with wax paper.

Microwave at 50% (Medium) 3 to 7 minutes, or until sauce is hot
and cheese melts, rotating dish once.

Per Serving:
Calories: 280   Cholesterol: 100 mg.
Sodium: 327 mg.   Exchanges: 1½ vegetable, 4 low fat meat, ½ fat

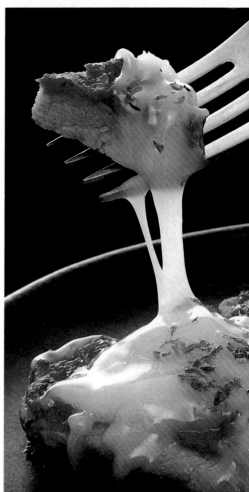

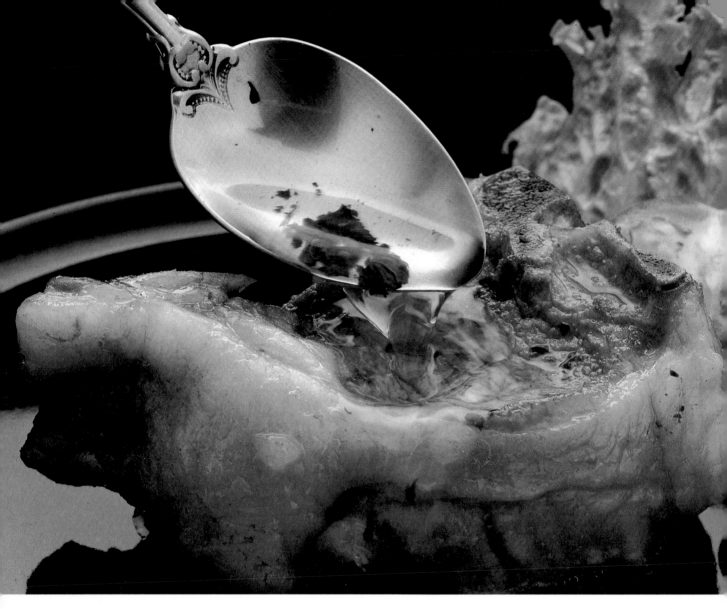

Lamb Chops With ▲ Mint Sauce

¼ cup Mint Sauce, page 129
4 lamb loin chops, 1¼-in. thick

Serves 4

Prepare Mint Sauce as directed. Set aside. Place chops on roasting rack. Spread 1 teaspoon mint sauce on each chop. Microwave at 50% (Medium) 7 to 10 minutes, or until chops reach desired doneness, rotating once. Spoon 2 teaspoons sauce over each chop before serving.

Per Serving:
Calories: 165
Sodium: 69 mg.
Cholesterol: 85 mg.
Exchanges: 3 low fat meat

Marinated Lamb Chops

¼ cup dry sherry
½ cup cider vinegar
2 green onions, finely chopped
2 tablespoons lemon juice
1 tablespoon lemon pepper
1 teaspoon Worcestershire sauce
1 teaspoon crushed rosemary leaves
½ teaspoon parsley flakes
¼ teaspoon grated lemon peel
½ teaspoon bouquet sauce, optional
4 lamb loin chops, 1¼-in. thick

Serves 4

Combine all ingredients except lamb chops in small bowl. Place chops in plastic bag, pour in marinade and seal. Marinate in refrigerator overnight.

Arrange lamb chops on roasting rack. Discard marinade. Microwave at High 5 minutes. Turn chops over. Reduce power to 50% (Medium). Microwave 7 to 9 minutes, or until lamb chops have reached desired doneness.

Per Serving:
Calories: 193
Sodium: 144 mg.
Cholesterol: 85 mg.
Exchanges: 1 vegetable, 3 low fat meat

Marinated Lamb Kabobs

1 can (8 oz.) pineapple chunks
   in own juice, drained,
   juice reserved
1 tablespoon lemon juice
2 teaspoons soy sauce
¼ teaspoon ground ginger
¼ teaspoon dry mint leaves
1 lb. boneless lamb, cut into
   24 pieces
8 firm cherry tomatoes
½ medium green pepper, cut
   into eighths
4 wooden skewers, 12-in. long

Serves 4

In small bowl combine ⅓ cup
reserved pineapple juice, lemon
juice, soy sauce, ginger and
mint leaves. Stir in meat; cover.
Marinate overnight in
refrigerator. Remove meat;
discard marinade.

Alternate lamb, tomatoes,
green peppers and pineapple
chunks on skewers.

Arrange skewers on roasting
rack. Microwave at 50%
(Medium) 8 to 11 minutes, or
until lamb is desired doneness.

NOTE: for low sodium diet
substitute low-salt soy sauce.

Per Serving:
   Calories: 205
   Sodium: 234 mg.
   Cholesterol: 85 mg.
   Exchanges: 1 fruit, 3 low
                    fat meat

Lamb Stew With Italian Green Beans

1 lb. lean lamb shoulder,
    cut into ¾-in. cubes
2 tablespoons all-purpose
    flour
1 teaspoon salt, optional
¼ teaspoon pepper
1 can (16 oz.) whole tomatoes
¾ cup water
8 oz. sliced fresh mushrooms
1 medium onion, quartered
1 teaspoon instant beef
    bouillon granules
½ teaspoon dried basil
¼ teaspoon crushed rosemary
    leaves
1 pkg. (10 oz.) frozen
    Italian green beans

Serves 6

In 3-qt. casserole combine lamb, flour, salt and pepper. Stir to coat lamb. Add tomatoes, water, mushrooms, onion, bouillon, basil and rosemary. Stir to break apart tomatoes; cover.

Microwave at High 5 minutes. Reduce power to 50% (Medium). Microwave 20 minutes; stir and re-cover.

Microwave at 50% (Medium) 20 to 30 minutes longer, or until lamb is fork tender. Add Italian beans; cover.

Microwave at 50% (Medium) 10 minutes, or until beans are hot; stir. Let stand, covered, 5 to 10 minutes.

NOTE: for low sodium diet substitute low-salt bouillon.

Per Serving:
    Calories: 156
    Sodium: 540 mg.
    Cholesterol: 57 mg.
    Exchanges: 2 vegetable, 2 low
                     fat meat

Middle Eastern Lamb Meatballs

Meatballs:

1 lb. lean ground lamb
1 small onion, finely chopped
½ teaspoon dry mint leaves
½ teaspoon parsley flakes
½ teaspoon salt, optional
¼ teaspoon ground cinnamon
¼ teaspoon ground cumin
¼ teaspoon pepper

Sauce:

3 tomatoes, peeled and
   coarsely chopped
1 small onion, chopped
½ cup chopped green pepper
2 teaspoons olive oil
2 teaspoons parsley flakes
1 teaspoon salt, optional
¼ teaspoon garlic powder

Serves 4

Per Serving:
  Calories: 219
  Sodium: 828 mg.
  Cholesterol: 85 mg.
  Exchanges: 1 vegetable, 3 low
                   fat meat, ½ fat

How to Microwave Middle Eastern Lamb Meatballs

Blend meatball ingredients in medium bowl. Form into 12 meatballs. Place on roasting rack; cover with wax paper.

Microwave at High 3 minutes. Rearrange meatballs. Microwave 1½ to 2½ minutes longer, or until meat is no longer pink. Set aside.

Combine sauce ingredients in 12 × 8-in. baking dish; cover. Microwave at High 4 to 5 minutes, or until green pepper is tender. Add meatballs; cover. Microwave at High 1 to 2 minutes to reheat.

◄ Tongue Stew

2¼ to 2¾ lb. beef tongue
2¾ cups hot water, divided
 ½ teaspoon salt, optional
 ¼ teaspoon pepper
 2 teaspoons onion powder
 1 tablespoon cornstarch
 1 potato, peeled, cubed
 3 large carrots, thinly sliced
 ½ teaspoon garlic powder
 1 tablespoon Worcestershire
   sauce

Serves 4

Wash tongue and trim fat. Place in 3-qt. casserole with 1½ cups water, salt, pepper and onion powder; cover. Microwave at High 3 minutes. Reduce power to 50% (Medium). Microwave 70 to 80 minutes, or until tender, turning tongue after half the time. Let stand 5 minutes.

Reserve broth; skim fat. Plunge tongue into cold water. Remove skin, fat, gristle and bones. Cut into cubes. Set aside. Blend ¼ cup water and cornstarch; add to broth with remaining ingredients. Cover. Microwave at High 10 minutes; stir twice. Uncover. Microwave 8 to 10 minutes, or until tender; stir twice. Add 1 cup hot water and meat. Microwave 2 to 4 minutes, or until hot.

Per Serving:
Calories: 245
Sodium: 65 mg.
Cholesterol: 77 mg.
Exchanges: ½ bread, 3 low fat
meat, 1½ vegetable

Sweet & Sour Tongue ▲

2¼ to 2¾ lb. beef tongue
1½ cups hot water
 ½ teaspoon salt, optional
 ¼ teaspoon pepper
 2 teaspoons onion powder

Sweet & Sour Sauce:

 ½ cup water
 ¼ cup unsweetened
   pineapple juice
 2 tablespoons catsup
 1 tablespoon cider vinegar
 2 teaspoons cornstarch

Serves 4

Wash tongue and trim fat. Place in 3-qt. casserole with water, salt, pepper and onion powder; cover. Microwave at High 3 minutes. Reduce power to 50% (Medium). Microwave 40 minutes. Turn tongue; cover. Microwave 30 to 40 minutes, or until tender. Let stand 5 minutes.

Plunge tongue into cold water. Remove skin, fat, bones and gristle. Discard cooking liquid. Slice thinly. Set aside.

In 2-cup measure blend sauce ingredients. Microwave at High 3 to 6 minutes, or until thickened, stirring 2 or 3 times. Microwave tongue at High 1 to 3 minutes to reheat. Serve with sauce.

Per Serving:
Calories: 200
Sodium: 165 mg.
Cholesterol: 77 mg.
Exchanges: 1 fruit, 3 low
fat meat

Braised Chicken Livers

1 teaspoon instant chicken
    bouillon granules
¼ cup hot water
1 lb. chicken livers, rinsed
    and drained
2 stalks celery, sliced
2 tablespoons lemon juice
¼ teaspoon pepper

Serves 4

Mix bouillon with water. Place
livers and bouillon in preheated
browning dish. Stir until sizzling
stops. Add remaining
ingredients; cover. Microwave at
High 4½ to 6½ minutes, or until
tender, stirring twice.

NOTE: for low sodium diet
substitute low-salt bouillon.

Per Serving:
  Calories: 177
  Sodium: 305 mg.
  Cholesterol: 673 mg.
  Exchanges: ½ vegetable, 3
               low fat meat

Liver & Onions

1 lb. sliced beef liver
1 medium onion, sliced
    and separated into rings
1 teaspoon parsley flakes
½ teaspoon salt, optional
¼ teaspoon pepper
¼ cup white wine
1 teaspoon instant chicken
    bouillon granules
¼ teaspoon garlic powder

Serves 4

Arrange liver in 12 × 8-in. baking
dish. Top with onion rings. Combine remaining ingredients; pour
over liver. Cover with wax paper.
Microwave at High 5 minutes.
Reduce power to 50% (Medium).
Microwave 9 to 14 minutes, or
until tender, rearranging once.

NOTE: for low sodium diet,
substitute low-salt bouillon.

Per Serving:
  Calories: 177
  Sodium: 511 mg.
  Cholesterol: 279 mg.
  Exchanges: 3 low fat meat

Liver & Onions With Tomato & Green Pepper ▲

1 lb. sliced beef liver
1 small onion, chopped
1 medium green pepper, cut
  into thin strips
1 medium tomato, cut into
  wedges

¼ cup tomato juice
½ teaspoon salt, optional
¼ teaspoon pepper
¼ teaspoon garlic powder

Serves 4

Arrange liver in 12 × 8-in. baking dish. Top with onion, green
pepper and tomato. In 1-cup measure, combine tomato juice, salt,
pepper and garlic powder. Pour over vegetables and liver. Cover
with wax paper. Microwave at High 5 minutes. Reduce power to
50% (Medium). Microwave 12 to 15 minutes, or until liver is tender,
rearranging pieces halfway through cooking.

Per Serving:
  Calories: 181   Cholesterol: 279 mg.
  Sodium: 276 mg.   Exchanges: ½ vegetable, 3 low fat meat

Poultry

Chicken, turkey and Cornish game hens make excellent substitutes for red meat for dieters, since they are generally lower in both calories and cholesterol. Microwaving extracts more fat from poultry than does conventional cooking. By skimming pan juices before serving, you can further reduce fat content. Most of the recipes in this section use chicken and turkey with skin removed, because most of the fat is concentrated in or directly under the skin. When cooked covered or with a sauce, the meat will retain moistness and flavor.

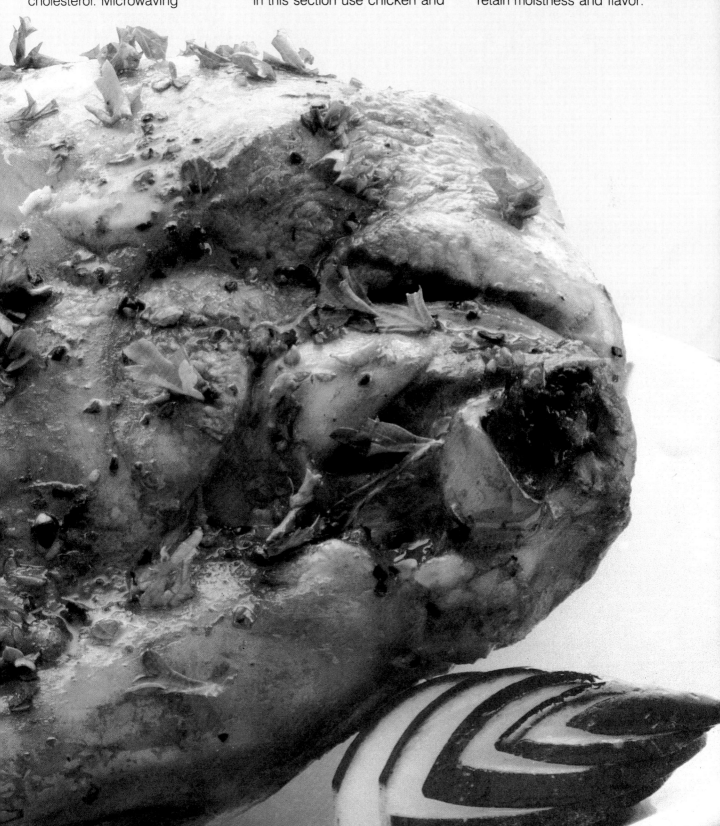

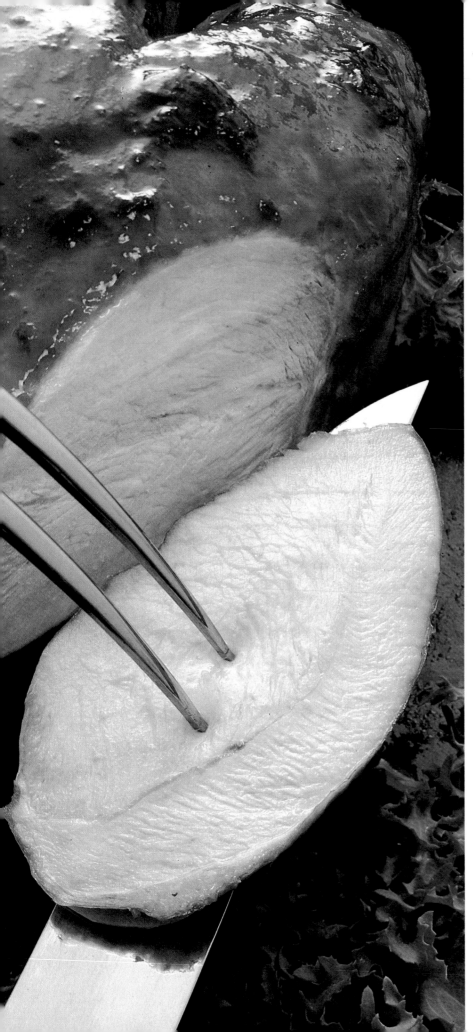

◀ Glazed Turkey Breast

5 to 6 lb. turkey breast
¼ cup low sugar tart cherry
　preserves
¼ cup low sugar imitation
　apple jelly

Serves 10

Cooking time: 11 to 15
　minutes per lb.

Place turkey breast-side down in baking dish. Estimate total cooking time; divide in half. Microwave at High 5 minutes. Reduce power to 50% (Medium). Microwave remainder of first half of time. Turn. Blend preserves and jelly. Glaze turkey with half of jelly mixture. Microwave for second half of time, or until internal temperature is 170°; glaze with remaining jelly during last 10 minutes.

Per Serving:
　Calories:　　188
　Sodium:　　75 mg.
　Cholesterol:　71 mg.
　Exchanges:　3½ low fat meat

Soy Turkey Drumsticks

2 turkey drumsticks
½ cup water
¼ cup soy sauce
1 tablespoon dry sherry
1 teaspoon fructose

Serves 2

Arrange drumsticks in 8 × 8-in. baking dish with meatiest portions to outside. Combine remaining ingredients; pour over drumsticks. Cover dish with plastic wrap. Microwave at High 3 minutes. Reduce power to 50% (Medium). Microwave 12 to 16 minutes, or until meat is tender and no longer pink; turn and baste every 3 minutes.

NOTE: for low sodium diet substitute low-salt soy sauce.

Per Serving:
　Calories:　　182
　Sodium:　　761 mg.
　Cholesterol:　60 mg.
　Exchanges:　½ fruit, 3 low fat
　　　　　　　meat

Orange Turkey Thighs▲

2 turkey thighs (2½ to 3 lbs.)
  skin removed
  Dash onion powder
  Dash pepper
⅓ cup orange juice
1 teaspoon soy sauce
1 teaspoon grated
  orange peel
¼ teaspoon coriander

Serves 4

Sprinkle both sides of turkey thighs with onion powder and pepper. Arrange bone side up in 12 × 8-in. baking dish.

In 1-cup measure combine orange juice, soy sauce, orange peel and coriander. Pour over thighs. Cover with wax paper.

Microwave at High 5 minutes. Reduce power to 50% (Medium). Microwave 20 to 30 minutes longer, or until meat is tender and no longer pink, turning and basting thighs twice during cooking. Cut meat from bone. Serve sauce with meat.

Per Serving:
  Calories: 173
  Sodium: 140 mg.
  Cholesterol: 60 mg.
  Exchanges: 3 low fat meat

Vegetable Braised Turkey▶

1 large tomato, coarsely
  chopped
1 large onion, sliced and
  separated into rings
1 large green pepper, cut
  into thin strips
2 turkey thighs (2½ to 3 lbs.)
  boned and skin removed
¼ cup hot water
½ teaspoon instant chicken
  bouillon granules
¼ teaspoon pepper
¼ teaspoon salt, optional
½ teaspoon red wine vinegar

Serves 4

Combine tomato, onion and green pepper in 8 × 8-in. baking dish. Place turkey thighs on top of vegetables with meatiest portions to outside of dish.

In 1-cup measure combine remaining ingredients. Pour over turkey and vegetables. Cover with plastic wrap. Microwave at High 3 minutes. Rotate and rearrange pieces. Reduce power to 50% (Medium). Microwave 30 to 35 minutes, or until meat is no longer pink, rotating and rearranging meat twice during cooking.

Per Serving:
  Calories: 184
  Sodium: 147 mg.
  Cholesterol: 60 mg.
  Exchanges: 1 vegetable, 3 low
                   fat meat

Turkey Casserole Pie ▶

Filling:

- 1 pkg. (10 oz.) frozen asparagus cuts
- 2 tablespoons water
- 2 tablespoons cornstarch
- 1 tablespoon instant chicken bouillon granules
- ⅛ teaspoon thyme
- ½ teaspoon salt, optional Dash pepper
- ¼ cup water
- ½ cup skim milk
- 1 small onion, coarsely chopped
- 1½ cups cooked, cubed turkey
- ⅔ cup grated carrot

Pastry:

- ¼ cup all-purpose flour
- ¼ teaspoon salt
- 1½ tablespoons shortening
- 1 to 1½ tablespoons water
- 1 to 2 drops yellow food coloring
  Paprika

Serves 4

NOTE: for low sodium diet substitute ½ teaspoon low-salt bouillon and omit salt in filling.

Per Serving:
Calories:	196
Sodium:	1830 mg.
Cholesterol:	18 mg.
Exchanges:	1 vegetable, 1 bread, 1 low fat meat, 1 fat

How to Microwave Turkey Casserole Pie

Place asparagus and 2 tablespoons water in 1-qt. casserole; cover. Microwave at High 5 to 7 minutes, stirring after half the time to break apart. Drain. Let stand, covered, while preparing pastry.

Toss flour and salt in medium bowl. Cut in shortening until particles resemble small peas. Combine 1 to 1½ tablespoons water and food coloring. Sprinkle just enough liquid over mixture to form a ball when stirred with fork.

Roll out on floured surface into 6-in. circle. Cut into quarters. Prick with fork. Place cutouts on wax paper. Sprinkle with paprika. Microwave at High 1 to 2 minutes, or until dry and flaky. Cool on wire rack.

Turkey Divan

1 pkg. (10 oz.) frozen
   broccoli spears
2 tablespoons water
1½ tablespoons all-purpose
   flour
¼ teaspoon salt, optional
⅛ teaspoon pepper
¼ teaspoon onion powder
¼ teaspoon parsley flakes
½ teaspoon dry mustard
1 tablespoon sherry
1 cup skim milk
½ cup shredded mozzarella
   cheese
6 to 8 slices cooked turkey
   Paprika

Serves 4

Place broccoli and 2 tablespoons water in 2-qt. casserole; cover. Microwave at High 6 to 8 minutes, stirring to break apart after half the cooking time. Set aside.

In medium bowl or 4-cup measure combine flour, salt, pepper, onion powder, parsley and dry mustard. Stir in sherry. Blend in milk. Microwave at High 3½ to 4 minutes, or until slightly thickened, stirring every minute. Blend in cheese until melted. Set aside.

Arrange broccoli in bottom of 8 × 8-in. baking dish. Split large spears in half lengthwise. Top with turkey slices. Pour sauce over turkey. Sprinkle with paprika. Reduce power to 50% (Medium). Microwave 4 to 6 minutes, or until thoroughly heated, stirring every 2 minutes.

Per Serving:
Calories:	200
Sodium:	236 mg.
Cholesterol:	57 mg.
Exchanges:	1 vegetable, 1 bread, 2 low fat meat

Combine cornstarch, bouillon and seasonings in medium bowl. Stir in water and milk. Add onion. Microwave at High 2½ to 4 minutes, or until sauce thickens and onion is tender, stirring after every minute.

Add turkey and carrot to asparagus in casserole. Stir in sauce. Microwave at High 3 to 5 minutes, or until hot and bubbly, stirring every 2 minutes. Top with pastry. Microwave 1 minute to reheat.

◄ Turkey Stew

¼ cup cold water
2 tablespoons cornstarch
2 cups cooked, cubed turkey
8 oz. sliced fresh mushrooms
1 medium onion, cut into
   8 wedges
1 pkg. (10 oz.) frozen peas or
   cut green beans
1¾ cups hot water
1 teaspoon parsley flakes
¼ teaspoon bouquet sauce,
   optional
⅛ teaspoon ground sage
¼ teaspoon pepper
1 tablespoon instant chicken
   bouillon granules
1 medium carrot, thinly sliced

Serves 6

In 3-qt. casserole blend ¼ cup cold water and cornstarch. Blend in remaining ingredients; cover. Microwave at High 20 to 30 minutes, or until sauce thickens and vegetables are tender, stirring 2 or 3 times.

NOTE: for low sodium diet substitute low-salt bouillon.

Per Serving:
Calories:	100
Sodium:	515 mg.
Cholesterol:	23 mg.
Exchanges:	2 vegetable, 1 low fat meat

Turkey & Squash ▲ in a Shell

2 medium acorn squash
2 tablespoons plain
   low fat yogurt
1 tablespoon brown sugar
¼ teaspoon nutmeg
¼ teaspoon salt, optional
⅛ teaspoon pepper
2½ cups cooked, diced turkey
⅛ teaspoon paprika

Serves 4

Pierce squash with fork. Microwave at High 10 to 16 minutes, or until fork tender; rearrange once or twice. Halve and discard seeds. Remove pulp, leaving ¼-in. shell. Reserve shell.

Place pulp in medium bowl. Blend in yogurt, sugar, nutmeg, salt and pepper. Stir in turkey.

Spoon squash mixture into shells. Arrange halves in 12 × 8-in. baking dish. Sprinkle with paprika. Reduce power to 50% (Medium). Microwave 6 to 8 minutes, or until heated, rotating dish once.

Per Serving:
Calories:	200
Sodium:	173 mg.
Cholesterol:	47 mg.
Exchanges:	½ fruit, 1 bread, 2 low fat meat

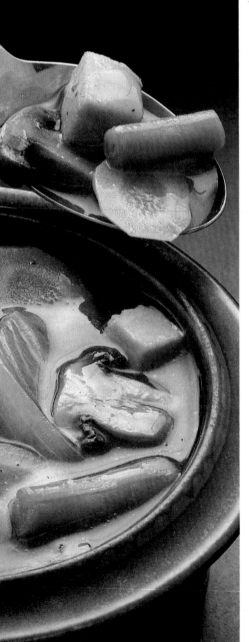

Sweet & Sour Turkey

1 pkg. (6 oz.) frozen
    pea pods
2 tablespoons water
1 small onion, thinly sliced
¼ cup chopped green pepper
1 large stalk celery, sliced
    diagonally
2 cups cooked, cubed turkey
1 can (15½ oz.) pineapple
    chunks, packed in own
    juice, juice reserved
4 teaspoons cornstarch
1 teaspoon instant chicken
    bouillon granules
    Dash ground ginger
¼ teaspoon salt, optional
1 teaspoon brown sugar
1½ tablespoons soy sauce
1 tablespoon vinegar

Serves 4

Place pea pods and water in 2-qt. casserole; cover. Microwave at High 2 to 3 minutes, or until defrosted. Break apart and drain. Stir in onion, green pepper, celery, turkey, and pineapple chunks. Set aside.

In 4-cup measure combine cornstarch, bouillon, ginger, salt and brown sugar. Stir in soy sauce, vinegar and pineapple juice. Microwave at High 2 to 3½ minutes, or until sauce is clear and thickened, stirring every minute.

Fold sauce into turkey mixture; cover. Microwave at High 4 to 6 minutes, or until heated through.

NOTE: for low sodium diet substitute low-salt soy sauce and bouillon.

Per Serving:
Calories:	188
Sodium:	534 mg.
Cholesterol:	35 mg.
Exchanges:	1 vegetable, 2 fruit, 1½ low fat meat

◄ Turkey Stuffed Tomatoes

4 large tomatoes
1 pkg. (10 oz.) frozen
   artichoke hearts
2 cups cooked, cubed turkey
1 tablespoon grated
   Parmesan cheese
¼ teaspoon garlic powder
¼ teaspoon marjoram
¼ teaspoon salt, optional
⅛ teaspoon pepper
   Paprika

Serves 4

Cut a thin slice from stem end of each tomato. Scoop out pulp. Pulp can be frozen for future use in sauces.

Place artichoke package in oven. Microwave at High 1½ to 4 minutes, or until package flexes easily. Drain. Chop artichokes into small pieces.

In medium mixing bowl combine artichokes, turkey, Parmesan, garlic powder, marjoram, salt and pepper. Spoon into tomato shells. Sprinkle with paprika. Place each tomato in custard cup or small bowl. Microwave at High 5 to 8 minutes, or until heated.

Per Serving:
Calories:	135
Sodium:	181 mg.
Cholesterol:	39 mg.
Exchanges:	2 vegetable, 1½ low fat meat

Turkey Chow Mein ►

2 turkey thighs (1¼ lbs. each)
   boned, cut into ½-in. cubes
2 tablespoons cornstarch
¼ cup water
2 teaspoons instant chicken
   bouillon granules
2 tablespoons soy sauce
1 cup thinly sliced celery
1 medium onion, chopped
1 can (16 oz.) chow mein
   vegetables, drained
8 oz. fresh sliced mushrooms
½ cup chow mein noodles

Serves 6

Place turkey pieces in 2-qt. casserole; cover. Microwave at High 5 to 6 minutes, or until meat is no longer pink, stirring after half the time. Drain.

Blend cornstarch and water. Add to casserole. Stir in all remaining ingredients except noodles; cover. Microwave at High 10 to 12 minutes, or until sauce thickens and vegetables are hot, stirring 2 or 3 times. Top with chow mein noodles.

NOTE: for low sodium diet use low-salt soy sauce and bouillon.

Per Serving:
Calories:	167
Sodium:	455 mg.
Cholesterol:	43 mg.
Exchanges:	1 vegetable, ½ bread, 2 low fat meat

Turkey Spaghetti Sauce

¼ cup water
1 can (6 oz.) tomato paste
1 can (16 oz.) whole tomatoes
1 small onion, finely chopped
1 medium carrot, grated

2 cups cooked, cubed turkey
¼ teaspoon rosemary
¼ teaspoon oregano
½ teaspoon salt, optional
⅛ teaspoon pepper

Serves 6

Combine all ingredients in 1½-qt. casserole. Break up tomatoes. Microwave at High 3 minutes. Reduce power to 50% (Medium). Microwave 10 to 15 minutes, or until thickened, stirring twice.

NOTE: If desired, serve over noodles, spaghetti squash or shredded zucchini. See Exchange Chart, pages 9 and 10.

Per Serving:
Calories:	104	Cholesterol:	23 mg.
Sodium:	205 mg.	Exchanges:	2 vegetable, 1 low fat meat

Fruit Stuffed Chicken

2 to 3 lb. broiler-fryer chicken,
 skin removed
1 teaspoon bouquet sauce
2 teaspoons water

Stuffing:
2 slices firm bread, cut into
 ½-in. cubes
1 medium apple, cored and
 cut into ½-in. cubes
1 small onion, chopped
¼ cup raisins
⅛ teaspoon pepper
 Dash salt, optional
¼ teaspoon ground sage
¼ teaspoon thyme leaves
½ teaspoon grated orange peel
1 stalk celery, chopped

Serves 6

Remove excess fat from chicken. Place breast-side down on microwave roasting rack. In small dish combine bouquet sauce and water. Brush chicken with half the bouquet mixture.

Microwave at High 5 minutes. Remove from oven. Tip chicken to drain liquid fat from cavity. Discard fat. Combine stuffing ingredients. Spoon into chicken cavity. Replace on rack breast-side up.

Brush with remaining bouquet sauce. Reduce power to 50% (Medium). Microwave 10 to 13 minutes per lb., or until legs move freely and internal temperature is 170°. Let stand, covered, 10 minutes.

Per Serving:
Calories: 269
Sodium: 159 mg.
Cholesterol: 90 mg.
Exchanges: ½ bread, 3 med.
                fat meat

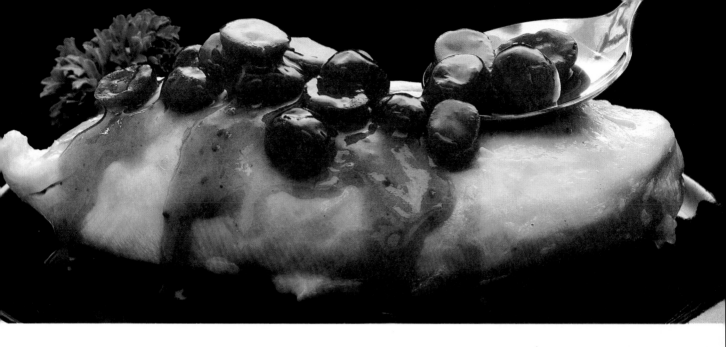

Cranberry Orange ▲ Glazed Chicken

⅔ cup freshly squeezed orange
  juice
⅔ cup fresh cranberries, halved
1 teaspoon sugar
2 teaspoons cornstarch
  Dash ground cloves
2 whole bone-in chicken
  breasts, halved, skin
  removed

Serves 4

In 2-cup measure combine all ingredients except chicken. Microwave at High 3 to 4 minutes, or until mixture thickens, stirring 2 or 3 times during cooking. Set aside.

Arrange chicken on roasting rack with meatiest portions to outside. Cover with wax paper. Microwave at High 5 minutes. Rearrange chicken. Microwave at High 3 minutes. Cover with one-third of glaze. Microwave at High 2 to 4 minutes longer, or until meat near bone is no longer pink. Serve remaining glaze over chicken.

Per Serving:
  Calories: 197
  Sodium: 90 mg.
  Cholesterol: 60 mg.
  Exchanges: 1 fruit, 3 low
                 fat meat

Lemon Seasoned ▶ Chicken Breasts

1 tablespoon water
½ teaspoon bouquet sauce
1 tablespoon lemon juice
1 teaspoon lemon pepper
½ teaspoon salt, optional
2 whole bone-in chicken
  breasts, halved, skin
  removed
1 to 2 teaspoons parsley
  flakes, optional

Serves 4

In small dish combine all ingredients except chicken and parsley. Arrange chicken breasts bone-side up on microwave roasting rack, with meatiest portions to outside of dish. Brush with half of seasoned mixture. Microwave at High 5 minutes.

Turn pieces over and brush with remaining mixture. Microwave 10 to 15 minutes, or until meat near bone is no longer pink, rotating once during cooking. If desired, sprinkle with parsley before serving.

Per Serving:
  Calories: 165
  Sodium: 132 mg.
  Cholesterol: 63 mg.
  Exchanges: 3 low fat meat

Chicken in Lemon Wine Sauce

3 medium carrots, sliced
2 stalks celery, sliced
3 green onions, chopped
1 tablespoon fresh, chopped parsley
2 tablespoons dry white wine
2 tablespoons lemon juice
½ teaspoon grated lemon peel
½ teaspoon basil leaves
¼ teaspoon thyme leaves
¼ teaspoon lemon pepper
½ teaspoon salt, optional
½ teaspoon instant chicken bouillon granules
2½ to 3 lb. broiler-fryer chicken, cut up, skin removed

Serves 4

NOTE: for low sodium diet substitute low-salt bouillon.

Per Serving:
Calories:	199
Sodium:	469 mg.
Cholesterol:	63 mg.
Exchanges:	1 vegetable, 3 low fat meat

How to Microwave Chicken in Lemon Wine Sauce

Combine all ingredients except chicken in 1-qt. casserole to make sauce; cover. Microwave at High 1 to 4 minutes, or until vegetables are tender-crisp, stirring after half the time.

Arrange chicken in 12 × 8-in. baking dish with meatiest portions to outside. Pour sauce over chicken. Cover with wax paper. Microwave at High 15 minutes; rearrange and baste with sauce every 5 minutes. Reduce power to 50% (Medium).

Microwave 4 to 10 minutes, or until vegetables are tender, basting 2 or 3 times. Skim fat from cooking liquid. If darker color is desired, brush chicken with mixture of ½ teaspoon bouquet sauce and 2 tablespoons water before serving.

Chicken Breast Cacciatore

1 can (16 oz.) whole tomatoes, cut up
½ medium green pepper, cut into thin strips
1 medium onion, sliced and separated into rings
¼ cup dry white wine
¼ teaspoon oregano leaves
½ teaspoon parsley flakes
¼ teaspoon salt, optional
2 whole bone-in chicken breasts, halved, skin removed
1 pkg. (7 oz.) vermicelli, cooked
2 tablespoons shredded Romano cheese

Serves 4

In 2-qt. casserole combine tomatoes, green pepper, onion, wine and seasonings; cover. Microwave at High 5 to 7 minutes, or until vegetables are tender, stirring once.

Arrange chicken in 12 × 8-in. baking dish with meatiest portions to outside of dish. Pour sauce and vegetables over chicken. Cover with wax paper. Microwave at High 14 to 18 minutes, or until chicken is tender and no longer pink; rearrange and spoon sauce over chicken twice during cooking time.

Serve chicken over vermicelli that has been tossed with Romano cheese.

NOTE: if desired serve over spaghetti squash. See Exchange Chart, page 9.

Per Serving:
Calories: 360
Sodium: 356 mg.
Cholesterol: 71 mg.
Exchanges: 1½ vegetable, 2 bread, 3 low fat meat

Tarragon Chicken

1 can (8 oz.) small onions, drained, juice reserved
¼ cup white wine
1 tablespoon fresh, chopped parsley
1 clove garlic, minced
1 teaspoon tarragon leaves
1 teaspoon instant chicken bouillon granules
Dash salt, optional
⅛ teaspoon pepper
1 tablespoon lemon juice
2 whole bone-in chicken breasts, halved, skin removed
1 teaspoon bouquet sauce
2 teaspoons water
4 thin slices lemon

Serves 4

In 12 × 8-in. baking dish, combine onion liquid, wine, parsley, garlic, tarragon, bouillon, salt, pepper and lemon juice. Arrange chicken, bone-side up, in dish. Combine bouquet sauce and water; brush half of mixture over chicken. Cover with wax paper. Microwave at High 5 minutes.

Turn over and rearrange chicken so least cooked portions are to outside of dish. Brush with remaining bouquet sauce mixture. Microwave 5 minutes, or until meat near bone is no longer pink. Add onions and place lemon slice on each piece. Microwave at High 1 to 2 minutes, or until onions are heated through. Spoon liquid over chicken before serving.

NOTE: for low sodium diet substitute low-salt bouillon.

Per Serving:
Calories: 183
Sodium: 417 mg.
Cholesterol: 63 mg.
Exchanges: ½ vegetable, 3 low fat meat

Mexican Chicken ▲

1 medium green pepper, thinly sliced
1 medium onion, sliced and separated into rings
8 oz. fresh sliced mushrooms
1 can (4 oz.) chopped green chilies, drained
2 whole bone-in chicken breasts, halved, skin removed
¼ teaspoon basil leaves
¼ teaspoon oregano leaves
Dash cayenne pepper
⅛ teaspoon garlic powder
1 can (15 oz.) tomato sauce

Serves 4

In 12 × 8-in. baking dish combine green pepper, onion, mushrooms and chilies. Cover with wax paper. Microwave at High 4 to 5 minutes, or until pepper is tender-crisp, stirring once. Drain.

Arrange chicken breasts over vegetables, bone-side up, with meatiest portions to outside of dish. Combine spices and tomato sauce. Pour half of tomato sauce mixture over chicken. Cover with wax paper. Microwave at High 10 to 16 minutes, or until chicken is opaque and tender. Turn over, rearrange and cover chicken with remaining sauce after half the time.

NOTE: if desired, serve over rice. See Exchange Chart, page 10.

Per Serving:
Calories: 260
Sodium: 229 mg.
Cholesterol: 63 mg.
Exchanges: 1 vegetable, 1 bread, 3 low fat meat

Citrus Marinated Chicken ▲

¼ cup lemon juice
1 tablespoon soy sauce
⅓ cup water
Dash pepper
⅛ teaspoon garlic powder
1 teaspoon grated orange peel
2 whole bone-in chicken breasts, halved, skin removed
4 slices orange
Fresh snipped parsley

Serves 4

In 2-cup measure combine lemon juice, soy sauce, water, pepper, garlic powder and orange peel to make marinade. Microwave at High 1 to 2 minutes, or until hot. Place with chicken in plastic bag. Refrigerate 1 to 2 hours. Arrange chicken in 12 × 8-in. baking dish with meatiest portions to outside. Top with orange slices. Pour marinade over chicken. Cover with wax paper. Microwave at High 13 to 18 minutes, or until meat is tender and no longer pink, rearranging and basting twice. Garnish with parsley.

NOTE: for low sodium diet substitute low-salt soy sauce.

Per Serving:
  Calories: 165
  Sodium: 329 mg.
  Cholesterol: 63 mg.
  Exchanges: 3 low fat meat

Raspberry-Lemon ▶ Sauced Chicken

2 whole bone-in chicken breasts, halved, skin removed
¼ teaspoon salt, optional
⅛ teaspoon pepper
1 cup fresh raspberries
¼ cup water
1 teaspoon sugar
1 teaspoon lemon juice
2 teaspoons cornstarch
4 slices lemon

Serves 4

Season chicken with salt and pepper. Place bone-side up on roasting rack with meatiest portions to outside of dish. Microwave at High 10 minutes, or until chicken is no longer pink, turning and rearranging pieces after half the cooking time. Set aside.

In small bowl combine berries, water and sugar. Slightly crush berries with fork. Stir in lemon juice and cornstarch. Microwave at High 1½ to 2½ minutes, or until mixture thickens, stirring once or twice. Microwave chicken at High 1 to 3 minutes, or until hot. Pour sauce over chicken. Garnish with lemon.

Per Serving:
  Calories: 195
  Sodium: 69 mg.
  Cholesterol: 63 mg.
  Exchanges: 1 fruit, 3 low fat meat

Chicken & Broccoli

3 tablespoons water
1 tablespoon soy sauce
1 tablespoon cornstarch
1 teaspoon fructose
1 teaspoon instant chicken
   bouillon granules
⅛ teaspoon garlic powder
1 tablespoon vegetable oil
3 medium green onions
2 whole boneless chicken
   breasts, skin removed,
   cut into strips
3 to 3½ cups fresh broccoli
   flowerets
4 oz. fresh sliced mushrooms

Serves 4

In small bowl combine water, soy sauce, cornstarch, fructose, chicken bouillon and garlic powder. Set aside.

Preheat 10-in. browning dish at High 5 minutes. Pour in oil. Add onions, chicken strips and broccoli. Stir until sizzling stops; cover. Microwave at High 3½ to 4½ minutes, or until chicken is no longer pink and broccoli is tender-crisp.

Add mushrooms and soy sauce mixture, stirring to coat chicken. Microwave 2 to 3 minutes, or until sauce thickens slightly, mushrooms are tender, and mixture is heated through, stirring 2 or 3 times.

NOTE: for low sodium diet substitute low-salt soy sauce and bouillon.

Per Serving:
Calories: 249
Sodium: 676 mg.
Cholesterol: 63 mg.
Exchanges: 1½ vegetable, 3
                 low fat meat, 1 fat

Lime Glazed Chicken

1 teaspoon grated lime peel
1 teaspoon lime juice
2 tablespoons dark rum
1 tablespoon sugar
¼ teaspoon instant chicken
    bouillon granules
½ cup water

2 teaspoons cornstarch
1 teaspoon bouquet sauce
2 teaspoons water
2 whole bone-in chicken
    breasts, halved, skin
    removed
4 lime slices

Serves 4

In 2-cup measure combine lime peel, lime juice, rum, sugar, bouillon, ½ cup water and cornstarch. Microwave at High 1 to 2 minutes, or until clear and thickened. Set aside.

In small dish combine bouquet sauce and 2 teaspoons water. Arrange chicken pieces bone-side up on roasting rack with meatiest portions to outside of dish. Brush with half the bouquet mixture. Microwave at High 5 minutes. Turn over and rearrange pieces; brush with remaining mixture. Place lime slice on each piece. Microwave at High 5 minutes, or until chicken is no longer pink. Serve with lime sauce.

NOTE: for low sodium diet substitute low-salt bouillon.

Per Serving:
    Calories: 195   Cholesterol: 63 mg.
    Sodium: 228 mg.   Exchanges: 1 vegetable, 3 low fat meat

Oriental Braised Chicken & Vegetables

2 whole boneless chicken
    breasts, skin removed, cut
    into strips
1 tablespoon soy sauce
1 can (8 oz.) water
    chestnuts, sliced, drained
1 can (8½ oz.) bamboo
    shoots, drained
1 cup bean sprouts, drained

1 cup chopped celery
4 green onions, chopped
8 oz. sliced fresh mushrooms
1 tablespoon cornstarch
1 tablespoon water
1 teaspoon instant chicken
    bouillon granules
½ teaspoon salt, optional

Serves 4

In 2-qt. casserole combine chicken and soy sauce. Microwave at High 3 to 4 minutes, or until chicken is opaque and no longer pink, stirring 2 or 3 times during cooking. Add water chestnuts, bamboo shoots, bean sprouts, celery, green onions and mushrooms.

Combine cornstarch, water, bouillon and salt. Stir into chicken mixture; cover. Microwave at High 10 to 13 minutes, or until vegetables are tender-crisp, stirring 2 or 3 times during cooking.

NOTE: for low sodium diet use low-salt soy sauce and bouillon.

Per Serving:
    Calories: 205   Cholesterol: 63 mg.
    Sodium: 581 mg.   Exchanges: 2 vegetable, 3 low fat meat

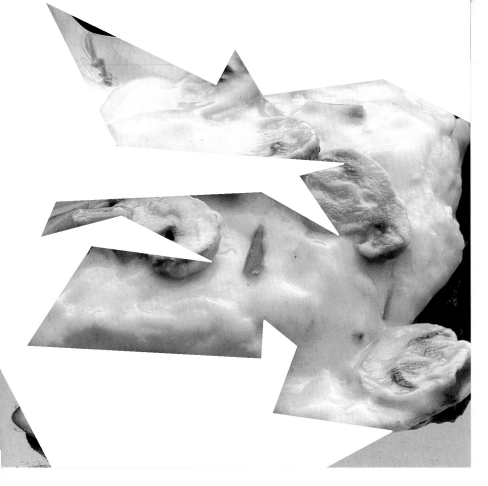

Chicken Asparagus Rolls ▶

¼ teaspoon garlic powder
¼ teaspoon rosemary
½ teaspoon salt, optional
2 whole boneless chicken
   breasts, halved, skin
   removed, pounded to flatten
2 slices (1 oz. each)
   mozzarella cheese, halved
1 pkg. (10 oz.) frozen
   asparagus spears,
   defrosted, drained
¼ teaspoon paprika
2 teaspoons grated Parmesan
   cheese

Serves 4

In small bowl combine garlic powder, rosemary and salt. Sprinkle over chicken. Lay ½ slice cheese on each piece.

Top with 4 asparagus spears. Fold long edges of chicken breast over asparagus; secure with wooden pick.

Sprinkle chicken rolls on all sides with paprika. Place seam side down in 12 × 8-in. baking dish. Cover with wax paper.

Microwave at High 3 minutes. Turn and rearrange chicken pieces. Sprinkle with Parmesan; cover. Microwave at High 2 to 4 minutes, or until chicken is opaque and tender.

Per Serving:
  Calories: 245
  Sodium: 368 mg.
  Cholesterol: 75 mg.
  Exchanges: 1 vegetable, 3 low
               fat meat

Chicken Breasts in Mushroom Sauce ▲

8 oz. fresh sliced mushrooms
¼ cup chopped green onions
1 tablespoon margarine or
   butter
2 tablespoons all-purpose flour
2 tablespoons dry sherry
¼ cup water

½ cup plain low fat yogurt
½ teaspoon salt, optional
   Dash pepper
1 teaspoon instant chicken
   bouillon granules
2 whole boneless chicken
   breasts, halved, skin
   removed

Serves 4

Combine mushrooms and onions in 1-qt. casserole. Cover. Microwave at High 3 to 4½ minutes, or until mushrooms are tender. Drain well. Place margarine in 4-cup measure. Microwave at High 30 seconds to 1½ minutes, or until melted. Blend in flour. Add sherry, water, yogurt, salt, pepper and bouillon. Stir in mushrooms and onions.

Arrange chicken in 8 × 8-in. baking dish. Pour sauce over chicken. Cover with wax paper. Reduce power to 50% (Medium). Microwave 14 to 20 minutes, or until sauce thickens and chicken is tender and no longer pink. Turn and rearrange breasts and stir sauce every 5 minutes during cooking. Serve sauce over chicken.

NOTE: for low sodium diet substitute low-salt bouillon.

Per Serving:
  Calories: 249   Cholesterol: 65 mg.
  Sodium: 527 mg. Exchanges: 1 vegetable, 3 low fat meat, 1 fat

Broccoli Chicken Rolls

2 slices (¾ oz. each) low fat
   cheese
2 whole boneless chicken
   breasts, halved, skin
   removed, pounded to flatten
1 pkg. (10 oz.) frozen chopped
   broccoli, defrosted, drained
½ cup skim milk
1 tablespoon all-purpose flour
1 tablespoon white wine
1 teaspoon parsley flakes
¼ teaspoon pepper

Serves 4

Per Serving:
  Calories: 235
  Sodium: 196 mg.
  Cholesterol: 67 mg.
  Exchanges: 1 vegetable, 4 low
                    fat meat

How to Microwave Broccoli Chicken Rolls

Cut one cheese slice into 8 strips; place 2 strips on each chicken piece. Place one-fourth of broccoli over cheese in center of each piece.

Fold ends of chicken over broccoli and secure with wooden picks. Place rolls seam side down in 8 × 8-in. baking dish. Cover with wax paper.

Microwave at High 5 to 8 minutes, or until chicken is no longer pink, turning over and rearranging once or twice. Drain and set aside.

Blend milk, flour, wine, parsley and pepper in 2-cup measure. Microwave at High 1½ to 3 minutes, or until thickened, stirring 2 or 3 times during cooking. Cut up and add remaining cheese slice, stirring until sauce is smooth.

Pour sauce over chicken. Microwave at High 30 to 60 seconds, or until rolls are heated through.

Barbecue Chicken Drumsticks ▲

¼ cup chopped onion
2 tablespoons chopped
  celery
½ teaspoon sugar
½ teaspoon dry mustard
1 teaspoon Worcestershire
  sauce
1 tablespoon cider vinegar

¼ teaspoon liquid smoke
  flavoring
¾ cup catsup
⅛ teaspoon pepper
2 tablespoons water
8 chicken drumsticks, skin
  removed

Serves 4

Combine all ingredients except drumsticks in 4-cup measure. Cover with wax paper. Microwave at High 3 minutes, or until hot, stirring once. Reduce power to 50% (Medium). Microwave 13 to 19 minutes, or until vegetables are tender and flavors are blended, stirring every 2 or 3 minutes.

Arrange drumsticks on roasting rack with meatiest portions to outside. Brush with one-third of sauce. Cover with wax paper. Increase power to High. Microwave 7 minutes. Turn over and rearrange legs; brush with one-third of sauce; cover. Microwave at High 4 minutes. Brush with remaining sauce; cover. Microwave 1 to 4 minutes, or until meat is no longer pink and sauce is hot.

NOTE: for low sodium diet substitute low-salt catsup.

Per Serving:
Calories: 210   Cholesterol: 78 mg.
Sodium: 518 mg.   Exchanges: 1 fruit, 3 low fat meat

Arroz con Pollo ▲

1½ cups instant rice
⅔ cup water
1 medium tomato, chopped
1 small onion, chopped
⅓ cup chopped green pepper
1 clove garlic, minced
1 bay leaf
½ teaspoon salt, optional
¼ teaspoon black pepper
¼ teaspoon ground saffron
3 whole boneless chicken
  breasts, skin removed,
  cut into 1 × 2-in. pieces

Serves 6

In 2-qt. casserole blend all ingredients except chicken. Stir in chicken pieces; cover. Microwave at High 8 to 14 minutes, or until chicken is tender and no longer pink, and liquid is absorbed, stirring once or twice.

Per Serving:
Calories: 243
Sodium: 268 mg.
Cholesterol: 63 mg.
Exchanges: 1 bread, 3 low
       fat meat

Cornish Game Hens

2 Cornish game hens
   (1 to 1½ lbs. each)
1½ teaspoons bouquet sauce,
   optional
2 teaspoons water, optional

Serves 2

Cooking time: 7 to 9 minutes
per lb.

Place hens on roasting rack
breast side down. Mix bouquet
sauce with water and brush half
of sauce over hens, or use one
of the following glazes. Estimate
total cooking time. Microwave at
High for half the time. Turn hens
breast side up; rearrange. Baste
with remaining bouquet sauce
or glaze. Microwave at High for
remaining time, or until legs
move freely and juices run clear.

Per Serving:
Calories: 234
Sodium: 364 mg.
Cholesterol: 181 mg.
Exchanges: 3 med. fat meat

◄ Soy Garlic Glaze

2 teaspoons soy sauce
1 tablespoon white wine
   Water
1 teaspoon cornstarch
⅛ teaspoon garlic powder

Glazes 2 Cornish hens

In 1-cup measure combine soy
sauce and wine. Add water to
equal ½ cup. Blend in
cornstarch and garlic powder.
Microwave at High 1 to 3
minutes, or until thickened,
stirring once.

Baste 2 Cornish hens with half
of glaze. Microwave hens as
directed, basting again when
turning. Baste with any
remaining glaze before serving.

Per Serving:
Calories: 11
Sodium: 345 mg.
Cholesterol: 0
Exchanges: free

Vegetable Rice Stuffing ▲

½ cup thinly sliced carrots
1 cup thinly sliced celery
¼ cup chopped onion
½ cup cooked rice
¼ teaspoon thyme
⅛ teaspoon sage

Stuffs 2 Cornish hens

Combine all ingredients in 1-qt. casserole; cover. Microwave at High 1 to 3 minutes, or until celery is tender-crisp. Stuff 2 hens loosely and microwave as directed, opposite.

Per Serving:
Calories: 73
Sodium: 58 mg.
Cholesterol: 0
Exchanges: 1½ vegetable, ½ bread

Cherry Glaze ▲

⅓ cup low sugar tart red cherry preserves
Dash nutmeg

Glazes 2 Cornish hens

Microwave hens as directed, opposite, basting with bouquet mixture.

Blend preserves and nutmeg in 1-cup measure. Microwave at High 30 to 45 seconds, or until hot. Baste hens with glaze before serving.

Per Serving:
Calories: 69
Sodium: 0
Cholesterol: 0
Exchanges: 1½ fruit

Crab Meat Stuffing ▲

1 can (5 oz.) crab meat, rinsed and drained
½ cup chopped green pepper
1 teaspoon lemon juice
¼ teaspoon pepper
2 slices firm bread, torn into bite-size pieces

Stuffs 2 Cornish hens

Combine all ingredients except bread. Toss to blend. Stir in bread pieces. Stuff 2 Cornish game hens and microwave as directed, opposite.

NOTE: for low sodium diet, substitute well-drained frozen crab meat.

Per Serving:
Calories: 207
Sodium: 703 mg.
Cholesterol: 70 mg.
Exchanges: 1 bread, 2½ low fat meat

Fish & Seafood

Seafood is an excellent source of low fat protein. A pound of fillets goes a long way because there is no waste and little shrinkage. If you are watching cholesterol, avoid shrimp and substitute crab and other seafood which contain no more cholesterol than low fat meats. Microwaving is a superior way to prepare seafood, especially when you're on a diet. Fish can be microwaved without added fat, just until the flesh flakes or loses translucency. Overcooking toughens fish.

Grilled Tuna Steaks

1 lb. fresh tuna, cut into
  4 steaks

Serves 4

Remove skin from tuna. Preheat
10-in. browning dish at High 5
minutes. Add steaks. Microwave
at High 1 minute. Turn and rearrange. Microwave at High 1 to 3
minutes, or until fish flakes
easily and is no longer pink.

Per Serving:
Calories: 165
Sodium: 42 mg.
Cholesterol: 71 mg.
Exchanges: 3 low fat meat

Fish With Zucchini & Red Pepper

¼ cup minced celery
½ cup minced onion
½ cup shredded zucchini
1 tablespoon parsley flakes
2 tablespoons lemon juice
¼ teaspoon black pepper,
  optional
1 lb. fish fillets
1 small sweet red pepper, cut
  into thin strips

Serves 4

In small bowl combine celery,
onion, zucchini, parsley flakes,
lemon juice and black pepper.
Set aside.

Place fish fillets in 12 × 8-in.
baking dish. Top with vegetable
mixture. Arrange red pepper
strips over vegetables. Cover
with wax paper. Microwave at
50% (Medium) 10 to 15
minutes, or until fish flakes
easily with fork, rearranging
fillets once during cooking. Let
stand, covered, 2 to 3 minutes.

Per Serving:
Calories: 135
Sodium: 46 mg.
Cholesterol: 63 mg.
Exchanges: 1 vegetable, 2 low
                 fat meat

Sole Florentine ▲

2 pkgs. (10 oz. each) frozen
   chopped spinach
2 tablespoons dry minced
   onion
½ teaspoon grated lemon peel
½ teaspoon salt, optional
½ teaspoon pepper

½ teaspoon dry mustard
2 tablespoons grated
   Parmesan cheese
1 teaspoon parsley flakes
½ teaspoon paprika
1 lb. sole fillets

Serves 4

Place spinach packages in oven. Microwave at High 6 to 6½
minutes, or until package flexes easily. Rearrange once. Drain
spinach well. Place in 8 × 8-in. baking dish. Stir in onion, lemon
peel, salt, pepper and dry mustard. Spread spinach mixture evenly
over bottom of baking dish.

Combine Parmesan, parsley and paprika. Set aside. Place fish on
top of spinach mixture. Cover with wax paper. Microwave at High
4 minutes; rearrange and sprinkle with Parmesan mixture. Cover.
Microwave at High 2 to 6 minutes, or until fish flakes easily.

Per Serving:
  Calories: 155   Cholesterol: 70 mg.
  Sodium: 326 mg.   Exchanges: 2 vegetable, 2 low fat meat

Red Snapper

⅛ to ¼ teaspoon tarragon
   leaves
¼ teaspoon pepper
½ teaspoon onion powder
1 lb. red snapper
6 to 8 slices lime

Serves 4

Combine tarragon, pepper and
onion powder. Arrange fish in
8 × 8-in. baking dish. Sprinkle
with seasoning mixture. Cover
with wax paper. Microwave at
High 3 minutes; rearrange
pieces and top each with a
slice of lime; cover. Microwave
at High 2½ to 4½ minutes, or
until fish flakes easily.

Per Serving:
  Calories: 113
  Sodium: 40 mg.
  Cholesterol: 63 mg.
  Exchanges: 2 low fat meat

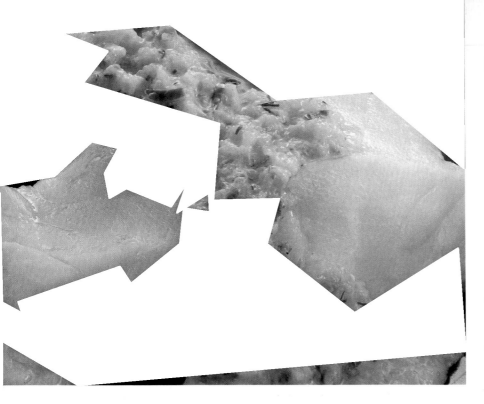

Parmesan Scallops

2 green onions, chopped
8 oz. sliced fresh mushrooms
1 clove garlic, minced
¼ cup white wine
2 tablespoons lemon juice
1 small bay leaf
1 teaspoon dry mustard
½ teaspoon instant chicken
  bouillon granules
1 tablespoon all-purpose
  flour
1 lb. scallops, rinsed and
  drained

Topping:
1 tablespoon dry bread
  crumbs
1½ teaspoons grated Parmesan
  cheese
½ teaspoon paprika
½ teaspoon parsley flakes

Serves 4

In 2-qt. casserole combine all
ingredients except scallops and
topping ingredients. Stir in
scallops; cover. Microwave at
50% (Medium) 7 to 10 minutes,
or until scallops are opaque
and flaky, stirring every 2
minutes. Remove bay leaf.

Divide scallops and cooking
liquid into 4 individual dishes.
Combine bread crumbs,
Parmesan, paprika and parsley
to make topping. Sprinkle
scallops with bread mixture.
Microwave at 50% (Medium) 1
to 2 minutes, or until heated.

NOTE: for low sodium diet
substitute low-salt bouillon.

Per Serving:
  Calories: 133
  Sodium: 416 mg.
  Cholesterol: 47 mg.
  Exchanges: 1½ vegetable, 2
                  low fat meat

Cod Fillets With ▲ Cucumber Dill Sauce

½ medium cucumber, thinly
  sliced
¼ teaspoon dill weed
2 green onions, chopped
¼ teaspoon salt, optional
½ cup plain low fat yogurt
1 lb. cod fillets
2 teaspoons lemon juice

Serves 4

Puree cucumber, dill, onions,
salt and yogurt in blender. Pour
into small bowl. Set aside.

Arrange fish on roasting rack.
Sprinkle with lemon juice. Cover
with wax paper. Microwave at
High 5 to 7 minutes, or until fish
flakes easily, rearranging after
half the cooking time. Set aside.

Reduce power to 50%
(Medium). Microwave cucumber
dill sauce 1 to 3 minutes to
heat. Serve over fish.

Per Serving:
  Calories: 117
  Sodium: 226 mg.
  Cholesterol: 59 mg.
  Exchanges: ½ vegetable, 2 low
                  fat meat

Trout With Lemon Stuffing

1 lb. trout fillets
2 tablespoons dry bread
  crumbs
½ cup chopped onion
½ cup chopped green pepper
4 oz. chopped fresh
  mushrooms
½ teaspoon salt, optional
¼ teaspoon pepper
½ to 1 lemon, sliced

Serves 4

Place trout in 12 × 8-in. baking
dish. In small bowl combine
bread crumbs, onion, green
pepper, mushrooms, salt and
pepper. Spread over fish, top
with lemon slices. Cover with
wax paper.

Microwave at High 5 to 7
minutes, or until fish flakes
easily. Let stand 3 to 5 minutes.

Per Serving:
  Calories: 133
  Sodium: 303 mg.
  Cholesterol: 62 mg.
  Exchanges: 1 vegetable, 2 low
                  fat meat

Easy Shrimp Creole ▲

1 can (16 oz.) whole tomatoes
1 medium onion, chopped
1 green pepper, chopped
½ teaspoon salt, optional
½ teaspoon pepper
½ teaspoon chili powder
1 medium bay leaf
1 lb. fresh shrimp, shelled
   and deveined

Serves 4

Combine all ingredients except shrimp in 1½-qt. casserole, breaking up tomatoes with spoon; cover. Microwave at High 8 to 12 minutes, or until green pepper is tender and sauce is bubbly, stirring once. Stir in shrimp; cover. Microwave at High 3 to 5 minutes, or until shrimp are just opaque, stirring once or twice. Do not overcook. Let stand 3 to 5 minutes. Remove bay leaf.

NOTE: if desired, serve over rice. See Exchange Chart, page 10.

Per Serving:
  Calories: 141
  Sodium: 345 mg.
  Cholesterol: 170 mg.
  Exchanges: 1½ vegetable, 2
                  low fat meat

Steamed Trout With ► Wine & Lemon

1 lb. trout fillets
4 slices lemon
¼ cup white wine
¼ cup chopped onion
1 teaspoon grated lemon peel
¼ teaspoon pepper
1 teaspoon parsley flakes

Serves 4

Arrange fish in 12 × 8-in. baking dish. Top with lemon slices. In 1-cup measure combine wine, onion, lemon peel, pepper and parsley. Pour over fish. Cover with wax paper. Microwave at High 4 to 7 minutes, or until fish flakes easily, rearranging after half the cooking time.

Per Serving:
  Calories: 128
  Sodium: 50 mg.
  Cholesterol: 62 mg.
  Exchanges: ½ vegetable, 2 low
                  fat meat

Crab Stuffed Sole

¼ cup chopped onion
¼ cup chopped green pepper
1 can (6 oz.) crab meat,
   rinsed and drained
2 tablespoons bread crumbs
½ teaspoon parsley flakes
½ teaspoon salt, optional
½ teaspoon lemon pepper
2 sole fillets (½ lb. each)
½ cup tomato juice
¼ teaspoon oregano leaves
¼ teaspoon basil leaves
½ teaspoon lemon juice
3 slices lemon, halved

Serves 6

NOTE: for low sodium diet use well-drained frozen crab meat.

Per Serving
Calories: 122
Sodium: 484 mg.
Cholesterol: 68 mg.
Exchanges: ½ vegetable, 2
               low fat meat

How to Microwave Crab Stuffed Sole

Combine onion and pepper in bowl. Microwave at High 3 to 5 minutes, or until tender; stir once during cooking.

Stir in crab, bread crumbs, parsley, salt and lemon pepper, to make stuffing. Set aside.

Arrange one sole fillet on roasting rack. Spoon on stuffing mixture; cover with second fillet. Set aside.

Mix tomato juice, oregano, basil and lemon juice to make sauce. Microwave at High 1 to 2 minutes, or until bubbly.

Pour ¼ cup sauce over fillets. Top with lemon slices. Cover with wax paper. Reduce power to 50% (Medium).

Microwave 11 to 15 minutes, or until bottom is flaky and center is hot, rotating after half the time. Serve with sauce.

Seafood Soup

1 medium onion, chopped
1 clove garlic, minced
1 stalk celery, chopped
¼ cup water
½ teaspoon instant chicken
 bouillon granules
1 cup white wine
1 cup tomato juice
1 lb. fish fillets, cut into
 1-in. cubes
2 tomatoes, cut into small
 wedges
2 teaspoons parsley flakes
⅛ teaspoon curry powder
⅛ teaspoon fennel seed
½ teaspoon thyme leaves
½ teaspoon ground sage
1 teaspoon salt, optional
¼ teaspoon pepper
1 lb. fresh shrimp, shelled
 and deveined
6 oz. cooked crab legs, cut
 into 2-in. sections

Serves 6

In 5-qt. casserole combine onion, garlic, celery, water and bouillon; cover. Microwave at High 4 to 6 minutes, or until onion is tender, stirring after half the cooking time. Stir in wine, tomato juice, fish, tomato wedges and seasonings; cover.

Microwave at High 10 to 12 minutes, or until fish is opaque and soup is hot, stirring once or twice. Mix in shrimp and crab meat; cover.

Microwave at High 4 to 5 minutes, or until shrimp are white and crab meat is hot, stirring after half the time. Let stand 2 to 3 minutes.

NOTE: for low sodium diet substitute low-salt bouillon and tomato juice.

Per Serving:
 Calories: 221
 Sodium: 274 mg.
 Cholesterol: 115 mg.
 Exchanges: 1 vegetable, ½
  bread, 3 low fat
  meat

Seafood Kabobs ▲

4 wooden skewers, 12-in. long
1 large green pepper, cut
 into 1-in. chunks
1 lb. scallops (about 22 to 25),
 halved
½ medium onion, cut into
 wedges
4 cherry tomatoes
2 tablespoons soy sauce
1 teaspoon lemon juice
¼ teaspoon garlic powder

Serves 4

On each of 4 skewers alternate green pepper chunk, scallop half and onion wedge, with a cherry tomato in the center of skewer. In small bowl combine soy sauce, lemon juice and garlic powder. Place skewers on roasting rack; brush with half of sauce. Cover with wax paper. Microwave at 50% (Medium) 12 to 15 minutes, or until scallops are opaque and pepper is tender; rearrange and brush with sauce after half the time.

NOTE: for low sodium diet substitute low-salt soy sauce.

Per Serving:
 Calories: 104
 Sodium: 807 mg.
 Cholesterol: 45 mg.
 Exchanges: ½ vegetable, 2 low
  fat meat

Hot Tuna Salad

2 stalks celery, chopped
2 green onions, chopped
1½ tablespoons lemon juice
¼ to ½ teaspoon dill weed
¼ teaspoon tarragon leaves
2 cans (7 oz. each) tuna
 packed in water, drained
1 jar (2 oz.) chopped
 pimiento, drained
2 tablespoons low calorie
 mayonnaise*
2 cups alfalfa sprouts
1 large tomato, cut into
 16 wedges

Serves 4

In 1-qt. casserole combine celery, onion, lemon juice, dill and tarragon; cover. Microwave at High 2½ to 5 minutes, or until celery is tender. Mix in tuna and pimiento. Microwave at High 3½ to 5 minutes, or until heated. Stir in mayonnaise. Serve over sprouts and tomato wedges.

*40 calories per tablespoon.

Per Serving:
 Calories: 165
 Sodium: 89 mg.
 Cholesterol: 58 mg.
 Exchanges: 1 vegetable, 2 low
  fat meat, ½ fat

Eggs & Cheese

Eggs and cheese, separately or in combination, provide an array of low calorie main dishes for lunch and dinner, as well as at breakfast time. Nutritionally, both make good meat substitutes because of their high protein content.

If you are avoiding cholesterol, you may use an egg substitute and you can still eat egg whites, since the saturated fat is concentrated in the egg yolk. Cooked egg whites offer the most complete form of protein available.

Cheese is an excellent source of both protein and calcium. Keep in mind that the fat and calorie contents of cheeses vary. Those made with skim or part-skim milk are good choices. For low cholesterol diets, use cheese substitutes.

Summer Lasagna

1 can (8 oz.) tomato sauce
1 medium onion, chopped
¼ teaspoon basil leaves
¼ teaspoon salt, optional
⅛ teaspoon pepper
¼ teaspoon oregano leaves
1 cup ricotta cheese
½ cup shredded mozzarella
    cheese
1 teaspoon parsley flakes
3 medium zucchini, about
    9-in. long
1 large tomato, sliced
2 tablespoons grated
    Parmesan cheese

Serves 6

Per Serving:
Calories: 129
Sodium: 283 mg.
Cholesterol: 19 mg.
Exchanges: 1½ vegetable,
               1 med. fat meat

How to Microwave Summer Lasagna

Combine tomato sauce, onion, basil, salt, pepper and oregano in small mixing bowl; set aside. In medium bowl combine ricotta, mozzarella and parsley. Set aside.

Peel zucchini and cut off ends. Slice zucchini lengthwise into strips. Arrange strips in 8 × 8-in. baking dish. Cover with wax paper.

Microwave at High 6 to 8 minutes, or until fork tender, rearranging after half the time. Drain liquid; place zucchini on paper towels to absorb excess moisture; cool slightly.

Layer 4 to 6 of the strips in the bottom of baking dish. Reserve 6 strips for second layer. Spread ricotta mixture over zucchini. Layer with sliced tomatoes.

Spread half of tomato sauce mixture over tomatoes; top with zucchini slices. Pour remaining sauce over zucchini and sprinkle with Parmesan.

Reduce power to 50% (Medium). Microwave, uncovered, 20 to 25 minutes, or until zucchini is tender and mixture is hot in center. Let stand 5 minutes before serving.

Breakfast Quiche

  4 slices firm white bread
  1 tablespoon margarine
    or butter
  2 to 3 tablespoons cold water
12 oz. sliced fresh mushrooms
  3 eggs, slightly beaten
½ cup evaporated skim milk
⅓ cup chopped green onions
  2 teaspoons fresh snipped
    parsley
¼ teaspoon dry mustard
¼ teaspoon pepper

Serves 4

Per Serving:
Calories:	195
Sodium:	190 mg.
Cholesterol:	191 mg.
Exchanges:	1 vegetable, 1 bread, 1 low fat meat, 1 fat

How to Microwave Breakfast Quiche

Chop bread into fine crumbs using blender or food processor. Blend in margarine thoroughly. Add enough water to form moist dough.

Press dough into pie dish to form crust. Microwave at High 1½ to 2½ minutes, or until sides appear dry. Set aside.

Place mushrooms in 1-qt. casserole. Microwave at High 5 to 7 minutes, or until tender, stirring once or twice. Drain thoroughly. Spread in shell.

Blend eggs and remaining ingredients in 1-qt. casserole. Reduce power to 50% (Medium). Microwave 1 minute. Stir.

Microwave 1 to 2 minutes, or until hot but not set, stirring every 30 seconds. Pour egg mixture over mushrooms.

Reduce power to 30% (Low). Microwave 7 to 14 minutes, or until soft set, rotating 4 times. Let stand 5 to 10 minutes.

104

Baked Cheese Sandwich ▲

8 slices firm white bread
4 slices (¾ oz. each) low fat
   American cheese
2 eggs, slightly beaten
1 cup skim milk
1 tablespoon instant minced
   onion

1 teaspoon prepared mustard
1 teaspoon parsley flakes
¼ teaspoon paprika
⅛ teaspoon black pepper
⅛ teaspoon cayenne pepper,
   optional

Serves 4

In 8 × 8-in. baking dish place 4 slices bread. Top each slice with a slice of cheese and the remaining bread. In 2-cup measure blend remaining ingredients. Pour over sandwiches. Place plastic wrap directly on sandwich surface. Refrigerate 8 hours or overnight.

Microwave, uncovered, at 50% (Medium) 6 minutes. Rotate each sandwich ½ turn. Microwave 6 to 10 minutes longer, or until sandwiches are set.

NOTE: If desired, 2 eggs may be replaced with ½ cup egg substitute; and a low sodium cheese product can be substituted for the American cheese.

Per Serving:
  Calories: 285   Cholesterol: 134 mg.
  Sodium: 485 mg. Exchanges: ¼ milk, ½ bread,
                                         1½ med. fat meat

Breakfast Soufflé

1 egg, separated
2 egg whites
½ teaspoon margarine or butter
2 drops yellow food coloring
2 tablespoons skim milk
¼ teaspoon basil leaves
¼ teaspoon salt, optional
⅛ teaspoon pepper

Serves 2

Beat 3 egg whites until soft peaks form. In deep cereal bowl microwave margarine at High 30 to 45 seconds, or until melted. Blend food coloring, egg yolk, milk, basil, salt and pepper. Fold into egg whites. Pour into cereal bowl. Reduce power to 50% (Medium).

Microwave 1½ to 3 minutes, or until mixture is set and no liquid can be seen in bottom of dish. Lift edge to check for liquid.

Per Serving:
  Calories: 78
  Sodium: 264 mg.
  Cholesterol: 127 mg.
  Exchanges: 1 med. fat meat

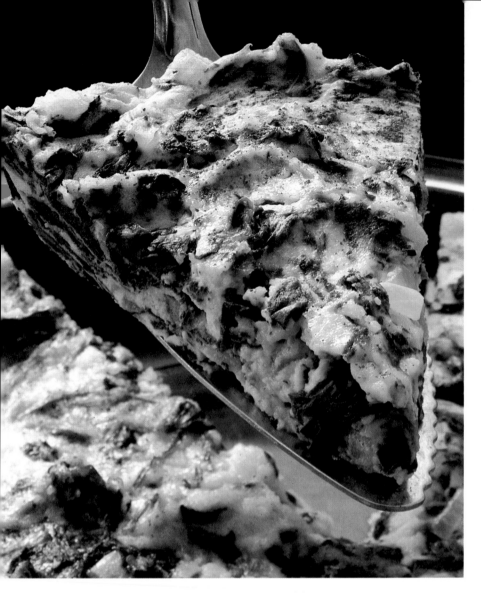

Open Face Omelet

2 teaspoons margarine or
  butter
4 large eggs, separated
¼ teaspoon salt, optional
⅛ teaspoon pepper

Serves 4

In 9-in. pie plate melt margarine
at High 30 to 45 seconds; set
aside. In medium bowl beat
egg whites until stiff but not dry.
In small bowl beat yolks lightly.
Add salt and pepper. Fold yolk
mixture gently into beaten
whites. Pour mixture into pie
plate. Reduce power to 50%
(Medium). Microwave 3 to 5
minutes, or until partially set. Lift
edges to spread uncooked portions. Microwave 2 to 3 minutes
longer, or until almost set, adding one of the toppings in the
following recipes, if desired.

Per Serving:
  Calories: 100
  Sodium: 155 mg.
  Cholesterol: 250 mg.
  Exchanges: 1 med. fat meat,
                   ½ fat

Crustless Ricotta Pie ▲

1 pkg. (10 oz.) frozen
  chopped spinach
½ cup chopped onion
2 eggs
1½ cups ricotta cheese

¼ teaspoon salt, optional
¼ teaspoon pepper
¼ teaspoon nutmeg
2 teaspoons all-purpose flour
⅛ teaspoon paprika

Serves 8

Combine spinach and onion in 1½-qt. casserole; cover. Microwave at High 4 to 6 minutes, stirring after half the time. Drain well.

In medium mixing bowl beat eggs with fork. Stir in ricotta, salt,
pepper, nutmeg and flour. Blend in spinach and onion. Spread
spinach mixture in 9-in. pie plate with rubber spatula. Sprinkle
with paprika.

Microwave at High 4 minutes, rotating every 2 minutes. Reduce
power to 50% (Medium). Microwave 3 to 11 minutes longer, or
until center is set. Let stand 5 minutes.

Per Serving:
  Calories: 61   Cholesterol: 66 mg.
  Sodium: 100 mg. Exchanges: 1 vegetable, ½ med. fat meat

Zucchini Tomato Omelet

Open Face Omelet, above
1 cup shredded zucchini,
  drained
½ cup chopped tomato
½ teaspoon onion powder
2 tablespoons plain low
  fat yogurt

Serves 4

Prepare Open Face Omelet as
directed. Combine remaining
ingredients. Spread over omelet
during last 1½ to 2 minutes of
cooking time.

Per Serving:
  Calories: 117
  Sodium: 155 mg.
  Cholesterol: 250 mg.
  Exchanges: ½ vegetable, 1
                   med. fat meat,
                   ½ fat

Broccoli Provolone Omelet▲

Open Face Omelet, opposite
½ cup chopped cooked
   broccoli, drained
1 oz. Provolone cheese, sliced
   into thin strips

Serves 4

Prepare Open Face Omelet as
directed. Place broccoli on
omelet; top with cheese strips.
Microwave 1 minute longer, or
until cheese melts.

Per Serving:
Calories:	120
Sodium:	172 mg.
Cholesterol:	254 mg.
Exchanges:	1 med. fat meat, 1 fat

Spiced Yogurt Omelet ▶

Open Face Omelet, opposite
¼ cup plain low fat yogurt
⅛ teaspoon ground nutmeg
½ teaspoon fructose

Serves 4

Prepare Open Face Omelet as
directed. Combine yogurt,
nutmeg and fructose. Spread
mixture over omelet during last
2 to 3 minutes of cooking time.

Per Serving:
Calories:	113
Sodium:	155 mg.
Cholesterol:	250 mg.
Exchanges:	1 med. fat meat, ½ fat

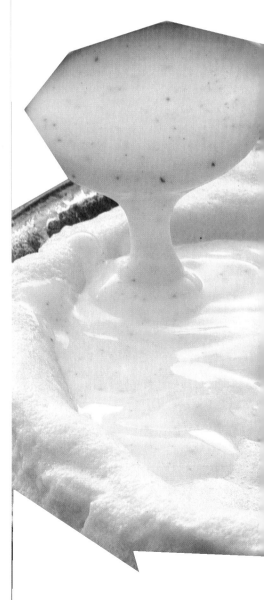

Soy Mushroom Omelet

Open Face Omelet, opposite
16 oz. fresh sliced mushrooms
2 tablespoons soy sauce

¼ teaspoon instant chicken
   bouillon granules
Dash onion powder

Serves 4

In small bowl combine mushrooms, soy sauce, bouillon and onion
powder. Microwave at High 3 to 4 minutes, or until mushrooms are
tender. Drain. Prepare Open Face Omelet as directed. Spread
mushrooms over omelet during last minute of cooking.

NOTE: for low sodium diet use low-salt bouillon and soy sauce.

Per Serving:
Calories:	113	Cholesterol:	250 mg.
Sodium:	807 mg.	Exchanges:	½ vegetable, 1 med. fat meat, ½ fat

Crab Meat Baked Eggs

1 can (6½ oz.) crab meat,
  rinsed and drained
3 slices (¾ oz. each) low fat
  American cheese
4 large eggs
  Dash paprika

                    Serves 4

NOTE: for low sodium diet use
well drained frozen crab and
low sodium cheese product.

Per Serving:
Calories: 196
Sodium: 592 mg.
Cholesterol: 298 mg.
Exchanges: 3 low fat meat,
               ½ fat

How to Microwave Crab Meat Baked Eggs

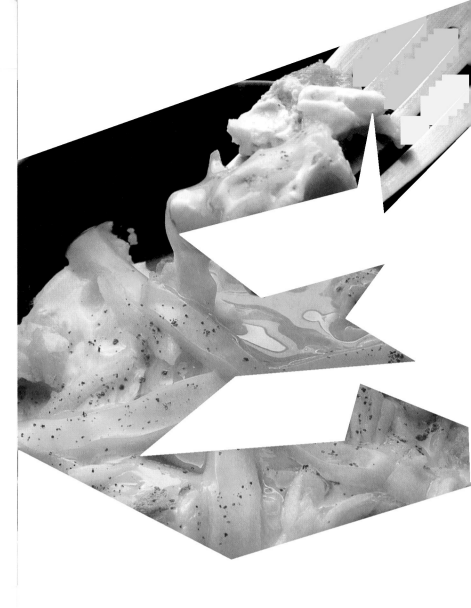

Flake crab. Reserve one-fourth.
Divide remainder into 4 custard
cups; form a well in each.
Quarter 2 cheese slices.
Arrange 2 quarters in each cup.

Break an egg into each
cheese-filled depression. Top
with remaining crab and strips
of last cheese slice. Sprinkle
with paprika. Cover each with
plastic wrap.

Microwave at 50% (Medium)
4½ to 5½ minutes for
soft-cooked eggs, or 5½ to 6½
minutes for hard-cooked.

Let stand, covered, 2 to 3
minutes until yolk is just soft
or hard set.

Mushroom Egg Foo Yung

3 large eggs
8 oz. sliced fresh mushrooms
⅓ cup chopped green onions
1 cup canned bean sprouts,
    drained
⅛ teaspoon pepper
1 can (4½ oz.) shrimp, rinsed
    and drained
1½ teaspoons cornstarch
2 teaspoons soy sauce
½ teaspoon instant chicken
    bouillon granules
½ cup water
1 teaspoon sugar

Serves 4

In medium bowl beat eggs well.
Stir in mushrooms, onion, bean
sprouts, pepper and shrimp.
Microwave at High 3½ to 5
minutes, or until mixture is soft
set, stirring 2 or 3 times. Cover
and set aside.

Preheat browning dish at High 5
minutes. Using a ½-cup
measure, place mixture on dish.
Push to form four patties. When
sizzling stops, turn patties over.
Microwave 1 to 1½ minutes, or
until firm and set. Cover and set
aside to keep warm.

In small bowl combine
cornstarch, soy sauce, bouillon,
water and sugar. Microwave at
High 2 to 3 minutes, or until
thickened, stirring once or twice
during cooking. Serve sauce
over patties.

NOTE: for low sodium diet
substitute low-salt soy sauce
and bouillon.

Per Serving:
    Calories: 138
    Sodium: 335 mg.
    Cholesterol: 240 mg.
    Exchanges: ½ vegetable,
                     2 med. fat meat,
                     ½ fat

Santa Fe Scrambled Eggs ▶

4 large eggs
¼ teaspoon parsley flakes
¼ teaspoon oregano
½ teaspoon salt, optional
⅛ teaspoon black pepper
¼ cup chopped green pepper
2 green onions, chopped
1 small tomato, chopped
¼ cup shredded mozzarella
    cheese

Serves 4

In medium bowl blend eggs
and spices. Stir in green
pepper, onions and tomato.
Microwave at High 3½ to 4
minutes, or until soft set, stirring
2 or 3 times during cooking.

Stir in mozzarella cheese; cover.
Let stand 1 minute, or until
cheese melts. Serve immediately.

Per Serving:
    Calories: 103
    Sodium: 287 mg.
    Cholesterol: 255 mg.
    Exchanges: ½ vegetable,
                     1 med. fat meat

Cheese Fondue ▶

8 oz. low fat American
    cheese, cut into 1-in. cubes
½ cup skim milk
1 to 2 teaspoons dry mustard
2 teaspoons Worcestershire
    sauce
1 teaspoon onion powder
1 teaspoon summer savory
2 tablespoons dry sherry

Serves 6

In large mixing bowl combine
all ingredients except sherry.
Microwave at 50% (Medium) 6
to 8 minutes, or until hot and
smooth, stirring 2 or 3 times
during cooking. Blend in sherry.
Serve with raw vegetables.

Per Serving:
    Calories: 83
    Sodium: 290 mg.
    Cholesterol: 14 mg.
    Exchanges: 1 low fat meat,
                     ½ fat

Vegetables & Fruits

Vegetables and fruits are a staple on many diets, both because of their relatively low caloric value and their nutrients. Microwaving enhances the preparation of these foods, allowing vegetables to retain their natural crispness, flavor and color. This means you don't have to add that extra butter or salt. Vitamins and minerals that are lost when you drain conventionally cooked vegetables aren't lost in microwaving.

Eating vegetables and fruits, alone or in combination with other foods, does not guarantee better health or weight loss. There is no scientific support for the notion that grapefruit burns fat, for example. They can however, be a valuable and tasty part of your diet. There are main and side dish recipes in this section, from plain to fancy. Use them in conjunction with the "free" vegetables which contain few calories when eaten raw.

Vegetable Chart

The microwave instructions are for fresh and frozen (not in butter sauce) vegetables. Canned vegetables are not included because some canning processes increase the caloric content of the vegetables, and some vitamins are discarded with the canning liquid before serving.

Vegetables contain no cholesterol and negligible amounts of sodium, so only calorie content is listed. Where sodium levels are significant, the amount is noted.

Very little water and no margarine or salt is needed to microwave vegetables. Microwave them at High in a covered dish or covered with plastic wrap. Keep covered during standing time.

Vegetable	Amount	Microwave Time	Standing Time	Procedure	Calories per Serving (½ cup)
Asparagus					
Fresh, spears	1 lb.	6½-9½ min.	3 min.	12 × 8-in. dish. Arrange in dish with tips toward center. ¼ cup water. Cover with vented plastic wrap. Rearrange after 4 min.	20 calories (6 spears)
Fresh, pieces	1 lb.	5-7 min.	3 min.	1 to 2-in. pieces. 2-qt. casserole. ¼ cup water. Stir once.	20 calories
Frozen, cuts	10 oz. pkg.	5-7 min.	3 min.	1-qt. casserole. 2 tablespoons water. Stir once.	20 calories
Frozen, spears	8 or 10 oz. pkg.	4½-5½ min.	3 min.	1-qt. casserole. 2 tablespoons water. Rearrange after half the cooking time.	20 calories (6 spears)
Beans					
Fresh, Green and Wax	½ lb.	12½-17½ min.	2-3 min.	1½ to 2-in. pieces. 1½-qt. casserole. ½ cup water. Stir every 4 min.	16 calories
Frozen, cuts	9 oz. pkg.	4-7 min.	3 min.	1-qt. casserole. 2 tablespoons water. Stir once.	16 calories
Beets*					
Fresh	1 lb. (5 medium)	17-19 min.	3-5 min.	Trim tops. 1½-qt. casserole. ½ cup water. Turn beets and rotate dish every 7 min. When fork tender, peel skins off.	27 calories
Broccoli					
Fresh, spears	1-1½ lbs.	8-12 min.	2-3 min.	12 × 8-in. baking dish. ½ cup water. Arrange in dish with heads toward center. Rotate after half the cooking time.	20 calories
Fresh, pieces	1-1½ lbs.	8-10 min.	3-5 min.	1-in. pieces. 2-qt. casserole. ½ cup water. Stir once.	20 calories
Frozen, spears, cuts, chopped	10 oz. pkg.	5-7 min.	3 min.	1-qt. casserole. 2 tablespoons water. Stir once.	20 calories
Brussels sprouts					
Fresh	1 lb.	4-8 min.	3 min.	1½-qt. casserole. ¼ cup water. Stir once.	26 calories
Frozen	10 oz. pkg.	5-7 min.	3 min.	1-qt. casserole. 2 tablespoons water.	26 calories
Cabbage*					
Fresh, Red and Green, wedges	1 lb.	10½-15½ min.	2-3 min.	4 wedges. Arrange like wheel spokes in 12 × 8-in. casserole. ¼ cup water. Rotate dish after half the cooking time.	15 calories
Fresh, Red and Green, shredded	1 lb.	7½-13½ min.	3 min.	¼-in. wide shreds. 1½-qt. casserole. 2 tablespoons water. Stir once.	15 calories
Carrots*					
Fresh, pieces	1 lb.	6-8 min.	3 min.	2-in. lengths. 1-qt. casserole. 2 tablespoons water. Stir once.	24 calories
Frozen, sliced	2 cups	4-7 min.	3 min.	1-qt. casserole. 2 tablespoons water. Stir once.	24 calories

Vegetable	Amount	Microwave Time	Standing Time	Procedure	Calories per Serving (½ cup)
Cauliflower					
Fresh, flowerets	2 cups	4-7 min.	2-3 min.	1½-qt. casserole. ¼ cup water. Stir after 3 min.	14 calories
Frozen	10 oz. pkg.	5-7 min.	3 min.	1-qt. casserole. 2 tablespoons water. Stir once.	14 calories
Corn					
Fresh, cob	1 ear	3-5 min.	5 min.	12 × 8-in. dish. ¼ cup water. Turn over and rearrange every 4 min.	70 calories (5-in. ear)
	2 ears	7-10 min.	5 min.		
	3 ears	6-12 min.	5 min.		
	4 ears	12-16 min.	5 min.		
Frozen, cob	½ ear	2½-3 min.	3 min.	12 × 8-in. dish. 2 tablespoons water. Turn over and rearrange once.	70 calories (5-in. ear)
	1 ear	5½-7½ min.	3 min.		
	2 ears	5-8 min.	3 min.		
	4 ears	10-12½ min.	3 min.		
Frozen, kernels	10 oz. pkg.	4-6 min.	3 min.	1-qt. casserole. 2 tablespoons water. Stir once.	69 calories
Mushrooms					
Fresh, sliced	8 oz.	3-6 min.	1-2 min.	8 × 8-in. dish. 2 tablespoons water. Stir once.	10 calories
Fresh, whole	8 oz.	3-4 min.	1-2 min.	1-qt. casserole. 2 tablespoons water.	10 calories
	16 oz.	3½-6½ min.	1-2 min.	2-qt. casserole. 2 tablespoons water. Stir every 1½ min.	10 calories
Peas*					
Fresh, shelled	2 lbs.	5-7½ min.	3 min.	1-qt. casserole. ¼ cup water. Stir once.	57 calories
Frozen	10 oz. pkg.	4-6 min.	3 min.	1-qt. casserole. 2 tablespoons water. Stir once.	57 calories
Pea Pods					
Fresh	4 oz.	2-4 min.	2 min.	9-in. pie plate. 2 tablespoons water.	43 calories
Fozen	6 oz. pkg.	3-4 min.	2 min.	1-qt. casserole. 2 tablespoons water. Stir once.	43 calories
Potatoes					
Baking	1	3-5 min.	5-10 min.	Scrub well; prick with fork. Arrange potatoes 1 inch apart on paper towel. Turn over and rearrange after half the time. Wrap in foil for standing time.	59 calories (1 medium)
	2	5-7½ min.	5-10 min.		
	3	7-10 min.	5-10 min.		
	4	10½-12½ min.	5-10 min.		
Boiling, sliced	4 medium	8-10 min.	3 min.	1 to 2-qt. casserole. ¼ cup water. Stir once.	59 calories (1 medium)
	6 medium	9-11 min.	3 min.		
Spinach*					
Fresh, whole leaves	1 lb.	5-8 min.	3 min.	3-qt. casserole. Stir once.	21 calories
Frozen, chopped leaves	10 oz. pkg.	7-9 min.	2-5 min.	1-qt. casserole. 2 tablespoons water. Stir once.	24 calories
Squash					
Acorn, fresh, whole (1½ lbs.)	1	8½-11½ min.	5-10 min.	Halve and remove seeds. Wrap each half with plastic wrap. Rotate and rearrange after half the time.	63 calories
	2	13-16 min.	5-10 min.		
Spaghetti, fresh, whole	1 lb.	4-6½ min.	5 min.	Pierce. Place on paper towels. After cooking, halve and remove seeds. Serve strands.	25 calories
Zucchini, fresh, sliced	2 cups	2½-6½ min.	3 min.	2-qt. casserole. 2 tablespoons water. Stir once.	13 calories
Frozen, mashed	12 oz. pkg.	5½-8 min.	2 min.	1-qt. casserole. Break apart after 2 min. Stir at 2 min. intervals.	65 calories
Tomatoes					
Fresh, whole	2 medium	1-3 min.	2 min.	Halve; space evenly in 9-in. round baking dish. Rotate and rearrange once.	32 calories (1 medium)
	4 medium	2½-4½ min.	2 min.		

*These vegetables contain sodium: Beets-46 mg.; Cabbage-72 mg.; Carrots-23 mg.; Peas-69 mg.; Spinach-46 mg.

◄ Crunchy Asparagus

1 pkg. (10 oz.) frozen
 asparagus cuts
2 tablespoons water
1 teaspoon lemon juice
3 to 4 drops tabasco sauce
1/8 teaspoon pepper
1/4 teaspoon salt, optional
1 tablespoon shelled sunflower
 seeds
 Lemon slices, optional

Serves 4

Place asparagus and water in
1-qt. casserole; cover.
Microwave at High 4½ to 5½
minutes, or until asparagus is
hot, stirring after half the
cooking time to break apart.
Drain. Cover and set aside.

In small bowl or 1-cup measure
combine lemon juice, tabasco
sauce and seasonings. Pour
mixture over asparagus. Toss to
coat. Sprinkle with sunflower
seeds. Garnish with lemon
slices if desired.

Per Serving:
 Calories: 32
 Sodium: 145 mg.
 Cholesterol: 0
 Exchanges: 1 vegetable

Green Bean Combination

1 lb. fresh green beans, cut
 into 1-in. pieces
8 oz. sliced fresh mushrooms
1/3 cup chopped red onion
1 clove garlic, minced
1/8 teaspoon pepper
1/4 cup water
1 tablespoon cider vinegar

Serves 4

Combine all ingredients except
vinegar in 2-qt. casserole; cover. Microwave at High 10 to 17
minutes, or until beans are tender, stirring every 3 minutes.
Drain. Toss with vinegar; serve.

Per Serving:
 Calories: 45
 Sodium: 0
 Cholesterol: 0
 Exchanges: 2 vegetable

Dilled Green Beans ▲

1 pkg. (10 oz.) frozen cut
 green beans
2 tablespoons water
1 green onion, finely chopped
2 teaspoons cornstarch
1/2 cup water

1/4 teaspoon dill weed
 Dash pepper
1 teaspoon cider vinegar
1 teaspoon instant chicken
 bouillon granules

Serves 4

Place beans and 2 tablespoons water in 1-qt. casserole; cover.
Microwave at High 4 to 7 minutes, or until beans are tender, stirring to break apart after half the time. Drain. Cover and set aside.

In small bowl or 2-cup measure blend remaining ingredients.
Microwave at High 1½ to 2 minutes, or until clear and thickened.
Pour over beans. Toss to coat.

NOTE: for low sodium diet substitute low-salt bouillon.

Per Serving:
 Calories: 38   Cholesterol: 0
 Sodium: 136 mg.   Exchanges: 1½ vegetable

◄ Harvard Beets

2 teaspoons cornstarch
¼ teaspoon salt, optional
  Dash pepper
  Dash ground cloves
2 tablespoons cider vinegar
1 can (16 oz.) sliced beets,
  drained, ⅓ cup liquid
  reserved
1 tablespoon orange juice

Serves 4

In 1-qt. casserole combine cornstarch, salt, pepper and cloves. Blend in vinegar, beet liquid and orange juice.

Microwave at High 1¾ to 2½ minutes, or until clear and thickened, stirring every minute. Add beets. Microwave at High 1 to 4 minutes, or until beets are thoroughly heated.

Per Serving:
  Calories: 40
  Sodium: 172 mg.
  Cholesterol: 0
  Exchanges: 1½ vegetable

Broccoli & Cauliflower ▲ With Mustard Sauce

2 cups fresh broccoli flowerets
2 cups fresh cauliflowerets
⅓ to ½ cup skim milk
1 tablespoon all-purpose flour
2 teaspoons prepared mustard
¼ teaspoon salt, optional
  Dash onion powder

Serves 4

Combine broccoli and cauliflower in baking dish. Cover. Microwave at High 8 to 11 minutes, or until tender, stirring once. Drain; set aside.

In medium bowl blend remaining ingredients with wire whip. Microwave at High 2 to 3 minutes, or until thickened, stirring every minute. Pour over vegetables. Toss to coat.

Per Serving:
  Calories: 50
  Sodium: 166 mg.
  Cholesterol: 0
  Exchanges: 2 vegetable

Italian Broccoli ▶
With Tomatoes

4 cups fresh broccoli flowerets
½ cup water
½ teaspoon oregano leaves
¼ teaspoon salt, optional
⅛ teaspoon pepper
2 medium tomatoes, cut
    into wedges
½ cup shredded mozzarella
    cheese

Serves 4

Place broccoli and water in
2-qt. casserole; cover.
Microwave at High 5 to 8
minutes, or until tender-crisp.
Drain. Stir in seasonings and
tomatoes. Microwave,
uncovered, at High 2 to 4
minutes, or until tomatoes are
hot. Sprinkle with mozzarella.
Microwave 1 minute, or until
cheese melts.

Per Serving:
  Calories: 100
  Sodium: 160 mg.
  Cholesterol: 9 mg.
  Exchanges: 2½ vegetable, ½
                high fat meat

Lemon Brussels Sprouts ▶

1 pkg. (10 oz.) frozen
    Brussels sprouts
1 tablespoon water
½ teaspoon lemon juice
⅛ teaspoon grated lemon peel
⅛ teaspoon salt, optional
    Dash pepper

Serves 4

In 1-qt. casserole combine
Brussels sprouts, water, lemon
juice and lemon peel; cover.
Microwave at High 3 minutes.
Stir to break apart; re-cover.
Microwave at High 2 to 3
minutes, or until Brussels
sprouts are tender. Drain;
sprinkle with seasonings.

Per Serving:
  Calories: 25
  Sodium: 63 mg.
  Cholesterol: 0
  Exchanges: 1 vegetable

◄ Mock Broccoli Soufflé

1 pkg. (10 oz.) frozen chopped
   broccoli
2 tablespoons water
1 egg, slightly beaten
1 tablespoon all-purpose flour
¼ cup plain low fat yogurt
½ cup low fat cottage cheese
½ teaspoon salt, optional
⅛ teaspoon pepper
4 oz. fresh mushrooms,
   coarsely chopped
3 green onions, finely chopped

Serves 4

Per Serving:
Calories:	95
Sodium:	265 mg.
Cholesterol:	67 mg.
Exchanges:	2 vegetable, ½ low fat meat, ½ fat

How to Microwave Mock Broccoli Soufflé

Place broccoli and water in 1-qt. casserole; cover. Microwave at High 5 to 8 minutes, stirring after 3 minutes to break apart.

Drain well and set aside. In small bowl blend together beaten egg, flour, yogurt, cottage cheese, salt and pepper.

Stir egg mixture, mushrooms and onions into broccoli. Reduce power to 50% (Medium).

Microwave 9 minutes, stirring every 3 minutes. Microwave 1 to 4 minutes longer, or until set.

Carrot Medley

4 cups thinly sliced carrots
1 small onion, sliced and
   separated into rings
1 teaspoon fresh, chopped
   parsley
1 teaspoon sugar
   Dash salt, optional
1 tablespoon margarine or
   butter
1 teaspoon instant chicken
   bouillon granules

Serves 4

Combine all ingredients in 1-qt. casserole; cover. Microwave at High 7 to 10 minutes, or until carrots are tender-crisp, stirring after half the cooking time.

NOTE: for low sodium diet substitute low-salt bouillon.

Per Serving:
Calories:	101
Sodium:	322 mg.
Cholesterol:	0
Exchanges:	2 vegetable, 1 fat

Rosemary Carrots ►

2 cups thinly sliced carrots
2 teaspoons instant chicken
    bouillon granules
2 tablespoons hot water
1 tablespoon brown sugar

¼ teaspoon dried rosemary,
    crushed
1 tablespoon chopped chives
⅛ teaspoon pepper

Serves 4

Place carrots in 2-qt. casserole. In small bowl or 2-cup measure combine bouillon, water, sugar and seasonings. Pour over carrots. Toss to coat; cover. Microwave at High 5 to 8 minutes, or until fork tender, stirring after half the cooking time.

NOTE: for low sodium diet substitute low-salt bouillon.

Per Serving:
    Calories: 65   Cholesterol: 0
    Sodium: 515 mg.   Exchanges: 1 vegetable, 1 fruit

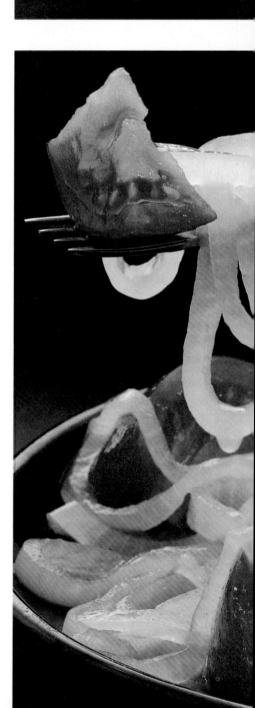

Company Cauliflower

½ medium head cauliflower,
    cut into flowerets
½ cup frozen peas
2 tablespoons water
2 tablespoons soy sauce
1 tablespoon lemon juice
1 tablespoon dry white wine
⅛ teaspoon ground ginger
4 oz. sliced fresh mushrooms

Serves 4

Combine cauliflower, frozen peas and water in 1-qt. casserole; cover. Microwave at High 5 to 8 minutes, or until cauliflower is tender-crisp. Let stand, covered, 2 to 3 minutes.

In 2-cup measure combine soy sauce, lemon juice, wine and ginger. Microwave at High 45 to 60 seconds, or until boiling. Stir in mushrooms. Drain cauliflower and peas. Add sauce mixture. Toss to coat; cover. Microwave at High 1 to 1½ minutes, or until mushrooms are tender.

NOTE: for low sodium diet substitute low-salt soy sauce.

Per Serving:
    Calories: 31
    Sodium: 258 mg.
    Cholesterol: 0
    Exchanges: 1 vegetable

Braised Onions ►
With Tomatoes

¼ cup hot water
1 teaspoon instant beef
    bouillon granules
2 tablespoons white wine
¼ teaspoon dry mustard
⅛ teaspoon pepper
    Dash salt, optional
⅛ teaspoon garlic powder
2 large white onions, sliced
    and separated into rings
1 small tomato, cut into
    8 wedges

Serves 4

In 1-cup measure combine hot water, bouillon, wine and seasonings. Place onion rings in 2-qt. casserole. Pour bouillon mixture over onions. Toss to coat; cover. Microwave at High 5 to 7 minutes, or until onions are tender, stirring after half the cooking time. Stir in tomato. Microwave at High 1 minute.

NOTE: for low sodium diet substitute low-salt bouillon.

Per Serving:
    Calories: 21
    Sodium: 241 mg.
    Cholesterol: 0
    Exchanges: 1 vegetable

Potato Toppers

Pizza Potato Topper

4 medium baking potatoes
½ lb.·extra lean ground beef
1 small onion, chopped
½ cup chopped green pepper
1 large tomato, chopped
2 tablespoons catsup
½ teaspoon salt, optional

Dash black pepper
Dash cayenne pepper
¼ teaspoon oregano
¼ teaspoon basil
½ cup shredded low fat
  mozzarella cheese

Serves 4

NOTE: for low sodium diet substitute low-salt catsup.

Per Serving:
Calories: 215   Cholesterol: 38 mg.
Sodium: 285 mg.   Exchanges: 1 vegetable, 1 bread, 1½ med.
                                     fat meat

Baked Potatoes

4 medium baking potatoes

Serves 4

Prick well-scrubbed potatoes twice with fork. Arrange 1 inch apart on paper towel on oven floor. Microwave at High 10½ to 12½ minutes, turning over and rearranging after half the time. Potatoes will feel slightly firm. Wrap in foil; let stand 5 to 10 minutes to complete cooking.

Per Serving:
Calories: 70
Sodium: 0
Cholesterol: 0
Exchanges: 1 bread

How to Microwave Pizza Potato Topper

Bake potatoes as directed, above. Let stand in foil while preparing topping. In 2-qt. casserole combine crumbled ground beef, onion and green pepper.

Microwave at High 3 to 4 minutes, or until beef is no longer pink. Stir once. Drain. Stir in tomato, catsup and seasonings.

Remove potatoes from foil. Split each in half lengthwise. Place on roasting rack. Lift and flake potato centers with a fork.

Spoon meat mixture over potatoes. Top with mozzarella. Microwave at High 1 to 2 minutes, or until cheese melts.

Curried Chicken Potato Topper

4 medium baking potatoes
¼ cup chopped green pepper
½ cup chopped celery
¼ cup chopped green onion
¼ cup shredded carrot
8 oz. sliced fresh mushrooms
½ teaspoon instant chicken bouillon granules
2 tablespoons all-purpose flour
¼ cup hot water
¾ cup skim milk
1 tablespoon white wine
1 teaspoon curry powder
¼ teaspoon poultry seasoning
¼ teaspoon salt, optional
2 cups cooked chicken, cut into ½-in. cubes
Fresh snipped parsley

Serves 4

Bake potatoes as directed, page 121. In 2-qt. casserole combine green pepper, celery, onion, carrot and mushrooms; cover. Microwave at High 3½ to 6 minutes, or until vegetables are tender-crisp. Drain liquid.

In medium bowl combine bouillon, flour and water. Blend in milk. Microwave at High 2½ to 5 minutes, or until slightly thickened, stirring after every minute. Stir in wine and seasonings. Add sauce and chicken to vegetables. Microwave at High 2½ to 4½ minutes, or until hot. Halve each baked potato lengthwise and flake center. Spoon topping over potatoes. Garnish with fresh parsley.

NOTE: for low sodium diet substitute low-salt bouillon.

Per Serving:
Calories: 354
Sodium: 298 mg.
Cholesterol: 16 mg.
Exchanges: 1 vegetable, 1 bread, 4 low fat meat

Ham Potato Topper

4 medium baking potatoes
¼ cup skim milk
2 tablespoons plain low fat yogurt
¼ cup hot water
½ teaspoon salt, optional
⅛ teaspoon pepper
¼ teaspoon onion powder
1 teaspoon parsley flakes
½ can (6¾ oz.) ham
Paprika

Serves 4

Bake potatoes as directed, page 121. Halve each baked potato lengthwise. Scoop out centers, leaving ¼-in. shell. Set shells aside. In medium mixing bowl combine potato, milk, yogurt, water, salt, pepper, onion powder and parsley. Beat until smooth and fluffy. Flake ham. Gently stir into potato mixture.

Pipe or spoon potato mixture into shells. Sprinkle with paprika. Arrange in 12×8-in. baking dish. Microwave at High 4½ to 6 minutes, or until thoroughly heated.

Per Serving:
Calories: 248   Cholesterol: 35 mg.
Sodium: 719 mg.   Exchanges: 1 bread, 1½ med. fat meat

Cheesy Turkey Potato Topper

4 medium baking potatoes
1 pkg. (10 oz.) frozen chopped broccoli
1 cup cooked turkey, cut into ¼-in. cubes
1 teaspoon instant chicken bouillon granules
½ teaspoon instant minced onion
¼ teaspoon dry mustard
⅛ teaspoon paprika
4 teaspoons all-purpose flour
¾ cup skim milk
2 slices low fat American cheese, each slice cut into 8 strips
Pimiento slices

Serves 4

Bake potatoes as directed, page 121. Microwave broccoli in package at High 3 to 4 minutes, or until warm, turning once. Drain broccoli well. Place in 2-qt. casserole. Stir in turkey. Set aside.

In medium bowl combine bouillon, onion, mustard, paprika and flour. Add milk slowly, using wire whip to eliminate lumps. Microwave at High 3 to 4 minutes, or until thickened, stirring several times. Combine milk mixture with turkey and broccoli. Halve each baked potato lengthwise and flake centers. Spoon one-fourth of topping over each potato, then top each with 4 strips of cheese. Garnish with pimiento slices. Microwave potatoes at High 30 to 60 seconds, or until cheese melts.

NOTE: for low sodium diet substitute low-salt bouillon.

Per Serving:
Calories: 207
Sodium: 372 mg.
Cholesterol: 22 mg.
Exchanges: 1 vegetable, 1 bread, 2 low fat meat

Beef & Mushroom Potato Topper

4 medium baking potatoes
½ lb. lean ground beef
1 medium onion, sliced and separated into rings
8 oz. sliced fresh mushrooms
1 clove garlic, minced
¼ cup skim milk

¼ cup tomato juice
2 tablespoons white wine
1 tablespoon cornstarch
½ teaspoon salt, optional
¼ teaspoon dry mustard
⅛ teaspoon pepper
Fresh snipped parsley

Serves 4

Bake potatoes as directed, page 121. In 2-qt. casserole combine ground beef, onion, mushrooms and garlic; cover. Microwave at High 3 to 6 minutes, or until meat is not pink, stirring twice. Drain.

Combine remaining ingredients except parsley. Stir into meat mixture. Microwave at High 4½ to 6½ minutes, or until thickened, stirring twice. Halve each baked potato lengthwise and flake centers. Spoon topping over potatoes. Garnish with parsley.

NOTE: for low sodium diet substitute low-salt tomato juice.

Per Serving:
Calories: 225   Cholesterol: 39 mg.
Sodium: 313 mg.   Exchanges: 1 vegetable, 1 bread, 1½ med. fat meat

◄ Ratatouille

½ lb. eggplant, cut into
    ½-in. cubes
1 clove garlic, minced
1 small onion, sliced and
    separated into rings
1 small zucchini, thinly sliced
½ medium green pepper,
    cut into thin strips
1 stalk celery, chopped
1 tomato, cut into wedges
    Dash pepper
¼ teaspoon salt, optional
¼ teaspoon basil leaves
¼ teaspoon oregano leaves
⅛ teaspoon thyme leaves
1 tablespoon grated Parmesan
    cheese

Serves 6

Combine all ingredients in 2-qt.
casserole; cover. Microwave
at High 7 to 10 minutes, or
until eggplant is translucent,
stirring 2 or 3 times.

Per Serving:
  Calories: 33
  Sodium: 105 mg.
  Cholesterol: 3 mg.
  Exchanges: 1 vegetable

Stewed Tomatoes

3 cups hot water
4 tomatoes
¼ cup chopped onion
½ teaspoon savory leaves
¼ teaspoon basil leaves
½ teaspoon salt, optional
⅛ teaspoon pepper
1 tablespoon grated Parmesan
    cheese

Serves 4

Measure water into 2-qt. bowl or
casserole. Microwave at High 6
to 10 minutes, or until boiling.
Immerse tomatoes and let stand
1 to 2 minutes, or until skins slip
off easily. Peel. Cut each tomato
into 1-in. cubes. Combine
tomatoes and remaining
ingredients in 2-qt. casserole.
Microwave at High 5 to 7
minutes, or until tomatoes soften
and mixture is of sauce-like
consistency, stirring twice.

Per Serving:
  Calories: 34
  Sodium: 274 mg.
  Cholesterol: 4 mg.
  Exchanges: 1 vegetable

◄ Zucchini With Pimiento

2 cups thinly sliced zucchini
    (2 medium)
1 jar (2 oz.) pimiento, drained
    and diced
½ teaspoon salt, optional
½ teaspoon basil leaves
1 small onion, chopped
⅛ teaspoon garlic powder
⅛ teaspoon pepper
¼ teaspoon imitation butter
    flavor

Serves 4

In 2-qt. casserole mix together
all ingredients; cover. Microwave at High 6 to 7 minutes, or
until fork tender, stirring once.

Per Serving:
  Calories: 25
  Sodium: 254 mg.
  Cholesterol: 0
  Exchanges: 1 vegetable

Stuffed Zucchini

1 slice bacon
2 medium zucchini
¼ cup minced onion
¼ teaspoon basil leaves
¼ teaspoon garlic powder
⅛ teaspoon black pepper
1 tablespoon grated Parmesan
   cheese
Dash cayenne pepper
½ cup chopped tomato
1 slice thin bread, toasted
   and crumbled

Serves 4

Per Serving:
Calories: 45
Sodium: 51 mg.
Cholesterol: 13 mg.
Exchanges: 1 vegetable, ½ fat

How to Microwave Stuffed Zucchini

Place bacon slice between double thickness of paper towels on oven floor.

Microwave at High 1 to 1½ minutes, or until crisp and browned. Crumble.

Halve zucchini lengthwise. Hollow out inside of each half, leaving ¼-in. shell.

Chop zucchini pulp and combine with bacon and remaining ingredients.

Fill zucchini halves with mixture, mounding slightly. Place in 12 × 8-in. baking dish.

Microwave at High 6 to 8 minutes, or until zucchini is tender. Do not overcook.

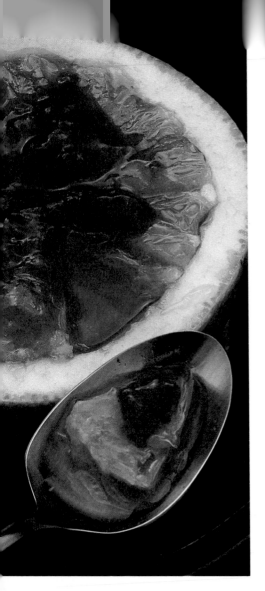

Baked Grapefruit

2 grapefruit
8 teaspoons low sugar
  strawberry spread
4 whole fresh strawberries,
  optional

Serves 4

Cut grapefruit in half. Loosen
each section. Top halves with
strawberry spread.

Microwave at High 4 to 6
minutes, or until grapefruit are
very hot, rotating after half the
time. Top each half with
strawberry in center.

Per Serving:
Calories: 62
Sodium: 0
Cholesterol: 0
Exchanges: 1½ fruit

Fruited Cheese Danish

2 eggs, slightly beaten
2 tablespoons skim milk
¾ teaspoon cinnamon, divided
½ teaspoon vanilla extract
4 slices firm white bread

2 teaspoons margarine or
  butter
½ cup cream style cottage
  cheese
1 cup sliced fresh
  strawberries

Serves 4

In shallow bowl blend eggs, milk, ½ teaspoon cinnamon and
vanilla. Soak bread in egg mixture. Place bread on wax paper.
Preheat 10-in. browning dish at High 5 minutes. Immediately add
margarine and bread. Microwave at High 1 minute. Turn slices
over. Microwave at High 2 to 4 minutes, or until bread is dry to
touch. Blend remaining cinnamon with cottage cheese. Spoon
one-fourth cottage cheese on each bread slice. Microwave at High
1 minute to melt cheese. Top each with ¼ cup sliced strawberries.

Per Serving:
Calories: 180   Cholesterol: 131 mg.
Sodium: 232 mg. Exchanges: 1 bread, 1 med. fat meat, 1 fat

Strawberry Rhubarb Compote

4 cups (20 oz. pkg.) frozen
   rhubarb, cut into 1-in.
   pieces
½ teaspoon cinnamon, optional
¼ cup water

2 cups sliced fresh
   strawberries
¼ cup fructose
5 to 7 drops red food coloring,
   optional

Serves 6

In 1½-qt. casserole combine rhubarb, cinnamon and water; cover. Microwave at High 10 to 14 minutes, or until rhubarb is tender, stirring 2 or 3 times. Mash rhubarb slightly. Stir in strawberries, fructose and food coloring.

Reduce power to 50% (Medium). Microwave 1 minute, or until strawberries are heated. For a sweeter compote, serve chilled.

Per Serving:
  Calories: 65   Cholesterol: 0
  Sodium: 16 mg.   Exchanges: 1 vegetable, 1 fruit

Apple Topping

4 cups diced apples
2 tablespoons fructose
½ teaspoon ground cinnamon
¼ teaspoon ground nutmeg
¼ teaspoon ground ginger

Serves 8

Stir all ingredients together in 1-qt. casserole. Microwave at High 4 to 6 minutes, or until apples are tender, stirring once or twice. Serve warm or cold.

NOTE: if desired, serve over toast or hot cereal. See Exchange Chart, page 10.

Per Serving:
  Calories: 40
  Sodium: 1 mg.
  Cholesterol: 0
  Exchanges: 1 fruit

Sauces

A colorful and lively sauce enhances the appearance and flavor of meats, poultry, fish or vegetables, especially in low fat or low sodium cooking. These sauces contribute appetite appeal with a minimum of added calories.

Tomato & Green Pepper Sauce Pictured on page 52

4 medium tomatoes, peeled and chopped
1 medium green pepper, cut into thin strips
1 small onion, chopped
½ teaspoon basil leaves
½ teaspoon salt, optional
¼ teaspoon oregano leaves
¼ teaspoon thyme leaves
¼ teaspoon marjoram leaves
⅛ teaspoon garlic powder
⅛ teaspoon black pepper
2 tablespoons water
1 tablespoon cornstarch

Serves 6
Serving size: ½ cup

In 1½-qt. casserole combine all ingredients except water and cornstarch. In small bowl blend cornstarch into water. Add to vegetable mixture. Cover. Microwave at High 5 minutes. Stir. Microwave at High 4 to 10 minutes, or until pepper is tender and sauce is slightly thickened, stirring once or twice. Serve with fish, meat or poultry.

Per Serving:
Calories: 31
Sodium: 169 mg.
Cholesterol: 0
Exchanges: 1 vegetable

Orange-Pineapple Sauce
Pictured opposite

1 can (8 oz.) crushed pineapple, packed in own juice
¼ cup low sugar orange marmalade
½ teaspoon parsley flakes

Serves 9
Serving size: 2 tablespoons

Combine all ingredients in 2-cup measure. Microwave at High 1½ to 3 minutes, or until marmalade melts. Serve over chicken or pork.

Per Serving:
Calories: 16
Sodium: 0
Cholesterol: 0
Exchanges: ½ fruit

Mushroom Sauce

8 oz. sliced fresh mushrooms
2 medium green onions, chopped
1 teaspoon instant beef bouillon granules
¼ teaspoon pepper
1¼ cups water
2 teaspoons cornstarch

Serves 5
Serving size: ¼ cup

In 1½-qt. casserole combine all ingredients except water and cornstarch. In small bowl blend cornstarch into water. Add to vegetable mixture. Cover. Microwave at High 3 to 6 minutes, or until mushrooms are tender and sauce is transparent, stirring once or twice. Serve with meat or fish.

NOTE: for low sodium diet substitute low-salt bouillon.

Per Serving:
Calories: 18
Sodium: 188 mg.
Cholesterol: 0
Exchanges: ½ vegetable

Sweet & Sour Sauce

½ cup unsweetened pineapple juice
5 tablespoons catsup
2 teaspoons vinegar
½ cup water
1 teaspoon instant minced onion

Serves 11
Serving size: 2 tablespoons

Combine all ingredients in 2-cup measure. Microwave at High 3 to 6 minutes, or until sauce is bubbly and onion is tender. Serve with beef, pork, chicken or vegetables.

NOTE: for low sodium diet substitute low-salt catsup.

Variation:
Barbecue Sauce: add 8 to 10 drops liquid hickory smoke flavoring.

Per Serving:
Calories: 11
Sodium: 82 mg.
Cholesterol: 0
Exchanges: free

Mint Sauce Pictured on page 62

⅔ cup water
1 teaspoon red wine vinegar
1½ teaspoons malt vinegar
2 teaspoons dry mint leaves
1 teaspoon sugar

Serves 8
Serving size: 1 tablespoon

Combine all ingredients in 2-cup measure. Microwave at High 1½ to 2½ minutes, or until boiling. Reduce power to 50% (Medium). Microwave 5 minutes, or until flavors blend. Use immediately or cover and refrigerate. Serve with lamb, pork, or vegetables.

Per Serving:
Calories: 0
Sodium: 0
Cholesterol: 0
Exchanges: free

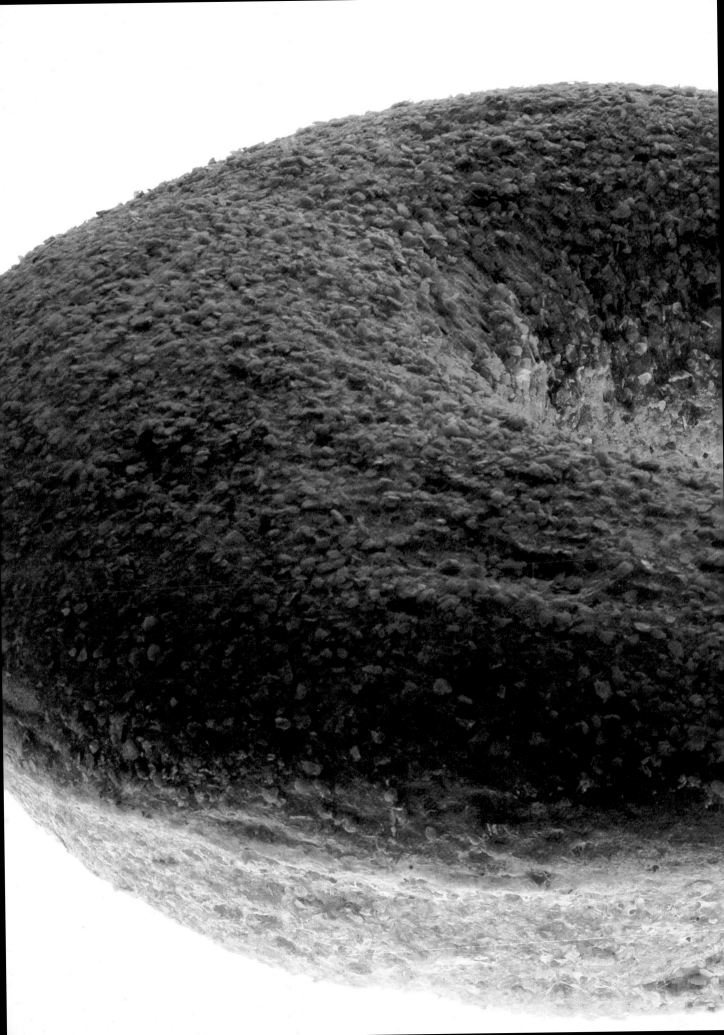

Breads

It's a myth that breads are fattening. The real culprit may be the high calorie spreads we put on them. These microwave breads are made with whole grains or other colorful ingredients and formulated to provide interesting flavor and texture when eaten "plain".

Four Grain Bread

1 cup whole wheat flour
½ cup rye flour
½ cup rolled oats
¼ cup corn meal
3 tablespoons light molasses
1 tablespoon vegetable oil
½ teaspoon salt
¼ cup warm water (105° to 115°)
1 cup boiling water
1 pkg. active dry yeast
1 to 1¼ cups white flour
  Skim milk
¼ cup wheat germ

Makes 24 slices
Serving size: 1 slice

Per Serving:
  Calories: 70
  Sodium: 42 mg.
  Cholesterol: 0
  Exchanges: 1 bread

How to Microwave Four Grain Bread

Blend whole wheat flour, rye flour, rolled oats, corn meal, molasses, oil, salt and boiling water in mixing bowl. Set aside.

Sprinkle yeast over warm water in 1-cup measure. Stir to dissolve. Stir into flour mixture.

Stir white flour gradually into mixture, adding just enough to make stiff dough.

Turn dough out on floured surface; with lightly greased hands, knead until smooth.

Knead by folding dough over toward you. Push with palms. Turn dough ¼ turn. Repeat, adding flour as needed.

Oil large bowl lightly. Place dough in bowl, turning to coat with oil. Cover loosely.

Let rise in warm place until light and doubled, about 45 to 90 minutes. Surface will be stretched and tight.

Test dough by pressing 2 fingers about ½ inch into it. If imprints remain, dough is doubled and risen.

Punch dough down; shape into ball. Turn dough out and cover with bowl. Let rest 15 minutes. Lightly oil 9-in. pie plate.

Shape dough into 18-in. strip. Brush with milk. Coat top and sides with wheat germ.

Sprinkle pie plate with remaining wheat germ. Shape dough, coated side up, into ring in pie plate. Pinch ends together.

Place lightly greased glass, open side up, in center of loaf. Let rise in warm place until doubled, 45 to 75 minutes.

Microwave at 50% (Medium) 6 minutes, rotating pie plate ½ turn after 3 minutes. Increase power to High.

Microwave 3 to 7 minutes, or until surface springs back when lightly touched, rotating pie plate once or twice.

Remove glass. Let stand 10 minutes. Transfer ring carefully to cooling rack.

Chewy Wheat Loaf

1 tablespoon lemon juice
  Skim milk
1 cup whole wheat flour
¼ cup brown sugar
1 teaspoon baking powder
1 teaspoon baking soda
¼ cup vegetable oil
2 eggs, slightly beaten
1 teaspoon cinnamon or
  pumpkin pie spice

Makes 24 slices
Serving size: 1 slice

In 1-cup measure combine lemon juice and enough milk to equal ½ cup. Stir.

Combine all remaining ingredients in medium mixing bowl. Stir in milk and lemon juice. Beat at low speed of electric mixer 1 minute. Line 9 × 5-in. loaf dish with wax paper cut to fit bottom. Add batter. Shield ends of loaf with 2½-in. wide strips of aluminum foil, covering batter with 1½ inches and molding remainder around handles of dish.

Microwave at 50% (Medium) 5 minutes, rotating dish once or twice. Increase power to High.

Microwave 1½ to 4 minutes, or until top of bread is firm to touch and almost dry, with a little moisture still visible. No uncooked batter should be visible through bottom of dish.

Let stand 3 minutes. Turn out of pan. Cut into 24 slices.

Per Serving:
  Calories: 66
  Sodium: 60 mg.
  Cholesterol: 21 mg.
  Exchanges: ½ bread, ½ fat

Five Grain Quick Bread

½ cup all-purpose white flour
½ cup whole wheat flour
¾ cup 40% bran cereal
½ cup quick-cooking rolled oats
2 tablespoons wheat germ
¼ cup corn meal
2 teaspoons baking powder
2 tablespoons vegetable oil
3 tablespoons brown sugar
⅔ cup skim milk
2 eggs

Makes 24 slices
Serving size: 1 slice

Per Serving:
Calories: 51
Sodium: 66 mg.
Cholesterol: 23 mg.
Exchanges: 1 bread

How to Microwave Five Grain Quick Bread

Blend all ingredients in medium mixing bowl. Line bottom of 9 × 5-in. loaf dish with wax paper. Spoon batter into dish.

Shield ends of loaf with 2½-in. strips of foil, covering batter with 1½ inches and molding remainder around handles.

Microwave at 50% (Medium) 6 to 11 minutes, or until bread tests done, rotating dish ¼ turn every 2 to 3 minutes.

Test by touching top lightly; it should spring back.

Look through bottom of glass baking dish; no unbaked batter should appear.

Let stand on counter 5 minutes. Turn bread out. Remove wax paper. Cut into 24 slices.

◀ Wheat Biscuits

¾ cup whole wheat flour
¾ cup all-purpose white flour
2½ teaspoons baking powder
¼ teaspoon salt
3 tablespoons margarine or
   butter
½ cup skim milk
1 teaspoon poppy seeds
1 tablespoon wheat germ

Makes 10 biscuits
Serving size: 1 biscuit

In medium mixing bowl combine flours, baking powder and salt. Cut in margarine until particles are fine. Add milk and stir until dough clings together.

Knead on lightly floured surface 12 times. Pat out to ¾-in. thickness. Top with poppy seed and wheat germ. Cut into 1½-in. circles. Place biscuits ½ inch apart on paper towels. Microwave at High 1½ to 2 minutes, or until dry and puffy, rotating ¼ turn every 30 seconds.

Variation:
Substitute ¼ cup rye flour, ¼ cup whole wheat and 1 cup white flour for original flours.

Per Serving:
Calories: 100
Sodium: 164 mg.
Cholesterol: 0
Exchanges: 1 bread, ½ fat

Spoon Bread ▲

½ cup skim milk
½ cup water
⅓ cup corn meal
1 tablespoon margarine or
   butter
½ teaspoon baking powder
¼ teaspoon salt
1 egg, separated
1 egg white

Serves 8

In 1-cup measure combine milk and water.

In small bowl combine ¾ cup of milk mixture with corn meal. Microwave at High 2 to 3 minutes, or until very thick; stir with wire whip 2 or 3 times. Blend in remaining milk, margarine, baking powder, salt and egg yolk.

In medium bowl beat egg whites until soft peaks form. Fold corn meal mixture into egg whites. Pour into 9-in. round cake dish. Place on inverted saucer. Reduce power to 50% (Medium). Microwave 6 to 9 minutes, or until center is set, rotating dish 2 or 3 times.

Per Serving:
Calories: 56
Sodium: 92 mg.
Cholesterol: 39 mg.
Exchanges: ½ bread, ½ fat

Caraway Orange Rolls

1 cup all-bran cereal
1 tablespoon vegetable oil
2 tablespoons light molasses
1 teaspoon grated orange peel
1 to 1½ teaspoons caraway
   seed, divided
½ teaspoon salt
¾ cup boiling water

1 pkg. active dry yeast
¼ cup warm water (105°
   to 115°)
2 to 2½ cups all-purpose
   white flour
2 teaspoons wheat germ
1 to 2 teaspoons skim milk

Makes 24 rolls
Serving size: 1 roll

Per Serving:
Calories:	21	Cholesterol:	0
Sodium:	46 mg.	Exchanges:	½ bread

How to Microwave Caraway Orange Rolls

Blend bran, oil, molasses, orange peel, ½ to 1 teaspoon caraway seed, salt and boiling water in medium mixing bowl. Cool until just warm.

Dissolve yeast in warm water. Stir into bran mixture. Stir in flour to make stiff dough. On floured surface, knead until smooth, about 8 minutes, adding flour as needed.

Cover loosely. Let rise until light and doubled in size, about 45 minutes to 1¼ hours. Punch down dough.

Divide into 24 pieces. Shape into balls. In small bowl combine ½ teaspoon caraway seed and wheat germ. Dip tops of rolls in milk, then in wheat germ mixture.

Arrange on 2 paper towel-lined dinner plates or 9 to 10-in. pie plates. Cover loosely. Let rise in warm place until light and doubled in size, about 45 minutes to 1½ hours.

Microwave, 1 plate at a time, at 50% (Medium) 6 to 8 minutes, or until tops spring back when lightly touched, rotating ¼ turn every 2 minutes.

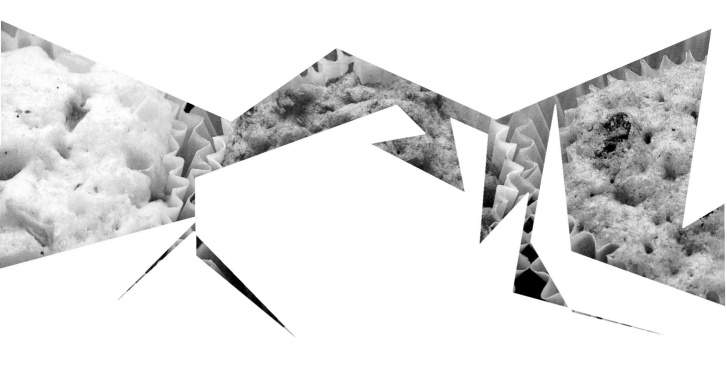

Vegetable Corn Muffins ▲

1 cup all-purpose white flour
½ cup cornmeal
1 tablespoon sugar
1 tablespoon baking powder
½ teaspoon salt
¾ teaspoon Italian seasoning
⅛ teaspoon garlic powder
2 eggs, beaten
1 tablespoon vegetable oil
½ cup corn, drained
⅓ cup skim milk
⅓ cup chopped green pepper
¼ cup finely chopped onion

Makes 12 muffins
Serving size: 1 muffin

Combine all ingredients in mixing bowl. Stir just until blended. Line each muffin or custard cup with two paper liners; fill half full. Microwave at High as directed below, or until top springs back when touched, rotating and rearranging after half the time.

1 muffin	¼ to ¾ minute
2 muffins	½ to 2 minutes
4 muffins	1 to 2½ minutes
6 muffins	2 to 4½ minutes

Per Serving:
Calories:	97
Sodium:	182 mg.
Cholesterol:	42 mg.
Exchanges:	1 bread, ½ fat

Carrot Bran Muffins ▲

1 cup 40% bran flakes
¾ cup skim milk
2 cups finely shredded carrot
1 cup whole wheat flour
2 tablespoons brown sugar
2 tablespoons vegetable oil
1 tablespoon lemon juice
1 teaspoon baking powder
½ teaspoon baking soda
¼ to ½ teaspoon cinnamon
¼ teaspoon salt
1 egg, slightly beaten

Makes 14 muffins
Serving size: 1 muffin

Combine bran, milk and carrot; let stand 5 minutes. Add remaining ingredients, stirring until particles are moistened. Line each muffin or custard cup with two paper liners; fill half full. Microwave at High as directed below, or until top springs back when touched, rotating and rearranging after half the time.

1 muffin	¼ to ¾ minute
2 muffins	½ to 2 minutes
4 muffins	1 to 2½ minutes
6 muffins	2 to 4½ minutes

Per Serving:
Calories:	86
Sodium:	87 mg.
Cholesterol:	18 mg.
Exchanges:	1 bread, ½ fat

Raisin Orange Muffins ▲

½ cup rolled oats
1 cup whole wheat flour
2 tablespoons vegetable oil
¼ cup sugar
2 teaspoons baking powder
¼ teaspoon salt
⅔ cup skim milk
2 eggs, slightly beaten
¼ cup raisins
½ teaspoon grated orange peel

Makes 12 muffins
Serving size: 1 muffin

Combine all ingredients in large mixing bowl. Stir just until particles are moistened. Line each muffin or custard cup with two paper liners; fill half full. Microwave at High as directed below, or until top springs back when touched, rotating and rearranging after half the time.

1 muffin	¼ to ¾ minute
2 muffins	½ to 2 minutes
4 muffins	1 to 2½ minutes
6 muffins	2 to 4½ minutes

Per Serving:
Calories:	113
Sodium:	100 mg.
Cholesterol:	42 mg.
Exchanges:	1 bread, 1 fat

Wheat Crackers

1 cup whole wheat flour
1 teaspoon caraway seed
¼ teaspoon salt
2 tablespoons margarine or
   butter
1 tablespoon vegetable oil
3 to 4 tablespoons water
   Corn meal or wheat germ

Makes 36 crackers
Serving size: 4 crackers

Per Serving:
Calories:	95
Sodium:	71 mg.
Cholesterol:	0
Exchanges:	1 bread, 1 fat

How to Microwave Wheat Crackers

Combine flour, caraway seed and salt in medium mixing bowl. With a pastry blender cut in margarine and oil until particles are fine.

Sprinkle water over mixture while tossing with fork until dough is just moist enough to hold together. Form dough into a ball.

Roll out on a floured pastry cloth to a 12 × 12-in. square. Prick generously with a fork. Cut into 36 squares.

Sprinkle large pie plate or microwave baking sheet with corn meal or wheat germ. Arrange half of crackers on baking sheet in circular pattern, placing 3 or 4 in center.

Microwave at High 2 to 3 minutes, or until dry and puffy, rotating twice. For crisper crackers, let cool on rack. Repeat with remaining crackers.

Desserts

If you love desserts, you don't have to give them up when you diet. With these recipes, you can have dessert and diet, too—choose from crêpes, soufflés, even a chocolate mousse. Fructose, either crystalline or liquid, is used as a sweetener in many of these recipes. It does contain calories, but is sweeter than sugar, so you use less of it. Fructose is available in health food stores and some supermarkets.

◄ Apricot Puff

1 can (16 oz.) apricot halves, packed in own juice, juice reserved
Water
2 tablespoons cornstarch
½ teaspoon vanilla extract
½ teaspoon grated lemon peel
1 egg yolk, beaten
3 egg whites

Serves 8

Per Serving:
Calories: 66
Sodium: 21 mg.
Cholesterol: 34 mg.
Exchanges: 1 fruit

How to Microwave Apricot Puff

Drain apricot juice into 1-cup measure. If needed, add water to equal 1 cup. Pour into 1-qt. casserole. Blend in cornstarch and vanilla. Chop apricots. Stir into liquid; add lemon peel.

Microwave at High 3 to 6 minutes, or until thick and translucent. Blend a small amount of apricot mixture into egg yolk. Stir back into apricot mixture. Set aside.

Beat egg whites until stiff peaks form. Gently fold in apricot mixture. Pour into 1½-qt. round casserole or soufflé dish.

Microwave at 30% (Low) 5 to 10 minutes, or until center is set, rotating dish every 2 to 3 minutes during cooking. Serve immediately.

Lemon Cheesecake

1 pkg. (8 oz.) Neufchâtel cheese
1 tablespoon fresh lemon juice
1 tablespoon grated lemon peel
2 eggs
¼ cup fructose
1 teaspoon graham cracker crumbs

Serves 6

In medium mixing bowl microwave cheese at 50% (Medium) 1 to 2 minutes, or until softened. Add lemon juice, peel, eggs and fructose. Beat at medium speed of electric mixer 2 minutes, or until well blended.

Pour into 9 × 5-in. loaf dish. Sprinkle graham cracker crumbs on top. Shield ends of dish with 2-in. wide strips of foil.

Microwave at 50% (Medium) 5 to 11 minutes, or until center is soft set, turning ¼ turn every 2 minutes. Chill.

Per Serving:
Calories: 177
Sodium: 39 mg.
Cholesterol: 155 mg.
Exchanges: 1 fruit, 2 med. fat meat

Hot Strawberry Ambrosia

Pictured on page 140

1 can (11 oz.) mandarin orange segments, drained
2 kiwi fruit, peeled and sliced
2 cups sliced strawberries
¼ cup papaya juice

Serves 4

Combine all ingredients in medium bowl. Microwave at High 2 to 4 minutes, or until fruit is heated, stirring 2 or 3 times.

Per Serving:
Calories: 86
Sodium: 3 mg.
Cholesterol: 0
Exchanges: 2 fruit

Tropical Chiffon

2 cans (8 oz. each) crushed
    pineapple, packed in own
    juice, juice reserved
    Water
1 tablespoon unflavored gelatin
2 eggs, separated
2 kiwi fruit, peeled, sliced into
    eighths

Serves 8

Measure pineapple juice into medium mixing bowl. Add enough water to equal 1¼ cups. Stir in gelatin. Microwave at High 1 minute, stirring to dissolve gelatin.

Beat egg yolks slightly. Stir in small amount of warm gelatin mixture. Blend back into the remaining gelatin.

Reduce power to 50% (Medium). Microwave 30 to 60 seconds, or until yolk mixture thickens slightly, stirring once. Refrigerate until soft set.

In medium mixing bowl beat egg whites until stiff peaks form. Beat yolk mixture until smooth; gently fold into egg whites.

Divide pineapple into 8 custard cups or small bowls. Cut kiwi fruit slices into quarters. Arrange 7 quarters of kiwi fruit over pineapple in each cup.

Top with the egg white mixture. Garnish each with one quarter of kiwi fruit. Chill before serving.

Per Serving:
Calories: 76
Sodium: 15 mg.
Cholesterol: 69 mg.
Exchanges: 1 fruit, ½ low
               fat meat

Lime Soufflé ▲

1 cup diet lemon-lime soda
2 tablespoons cornstarch
1 tablespoon lime juice
1 tablespoon grated lime peel
1 tablespoon fructose

2 to 4 drops green food
    coloring
1 egg yolk
3 egg whites

Serves 4

In small bowl or 2-cup measure combine diet soda, cornstarch, lime juice, peel, fructose and food coloring. Microwave at High 2½ to 3 minutes, or until thickened, stirring 2 or 3 times.

Beat egg yolk in small bowl. Stir 1 tablespoon of hot lime mixture into egg yolk; blend egg yolk mixture back into hot lime mixture. Set aside.

In medium bowl whip egg whites until soft peaks form. Fold lime mixture gently into whites. Pour into 1-qt. casserole. Reduce power to 30% (Low). Microwave 9 to 12 minutes, or until set, rotating ¼ turn every 2 minutes. Serve immediately.

Per Serving:
Calories: 61   Cholesterol: 69 mg.
Sodium: 46 mg.   Exchanges: ½ fruit, ½ med. fat meat

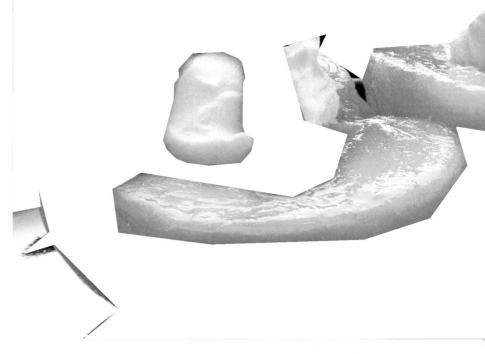

◄ Fruit Pie

1½ cups warm water
2 tablespoons unflavored gelatin
½ teaspoon lemon extract
½ teaspoon grated lemon peel
1 tablespoon fructose
½ teaspoon margarine or butter
2 tablespoons graham cracker crumbs
2 fresh peaches, peeled and sliced
2 cups sliced strawberries
2 cups fresh blueberries
Lemon slices

Makes 9-in. pie
Serves 6

In 4-cup measure combine water and gelatin. Microwave at High 1 to 1½ minutes, or until mixture is heated and gelatin dissolves. Stir in lemon extract, lemon peel and fructose. Set aside.

Butter a 9-in. pie plate. Sprinkle graham cracker crumbs over bottom and sides of plate.

Layer sliced peaches in pie plate. Top with one-third of gelatin mixture, then strawberries and blueberries. Cover with remaining gelatin mixture.

Refrigerate about 2 to 4 hours, or until completely set. Garnish with lemon slices.

Per Serving:
Calories: 98
Sodium: 10 mg.
Cholesterol: 0
Exchanges: 2 fruit, ½ low fat meat

Peach Melba ▲

4 fresh peaches, peeled, pitted and halved
Lemon juice
½ cup low sugar raspberry jam
1 cup prepared low calorie whipped topping

Serves 4

Arrange peaches in 12 × 8-in. baking dish. Brush with lemon juice to prevent discoloration. Cover with plastic wrap. Microwave at High 2 to 6 minutes, or until soft, rearranging after half the time. Cool.

Microwave jam in 1-cup measure at High 30 to 60 seconds, or until thinned, stirring once. Place 2 peach halves in each of 4 serving dishes. Top each with ¼ cup whipped topping, then 2 tablespoons jam. Serve immediately.

Variation:
Substitute 1 can (16 oz.) peaches for fresh. During first time span, microwave only until warm, not soft.

Per Serving:
Calories: 92
Sodium: 16 mg.
Cholesterol: 0
Exchanges: 2 fruit

Baked Apples

4 medium apples
⅓ cup diet raspberry soda
¼ teaspoon cinnamon

Serves 4

Core apples, leaving ½ inch of bottom intact. Place in custard cups. Combine soda and cinnamon in 1-cup measure. Spoon mixture into centers of apples. Cover each apple loosely with plastic wrap. Microwave at High 4 to 5½ minutes, or until apples are fork tender, rearranging and rotating apples after half the time. Let stand 2 minutes. Serve warm.

Variations:
Rum Baked Apples: Combine ⅓ cup diet cream soda, ½ teaspoon rum extract, ¼ teaspoon cinnamon and ⅛ teaspoon ginger for filling.

Maple Baked Apples: Combine ⅓ cup diet cream soda, ½ teaspoon maple extract, ¼ teaspoon nutmeg and ¼ teaspoon allspice for filling.

Per Serving:
Calories: 88
Sodium: 7 mg.
Cholesterol: 0
Exchanges: 2 fruit

Crêpes

1 cup all-purpose flour
1½ cups buttermilk or
    skim milk
1 egg, slightly beaten
¼ teaspoon salt, optional
    Vegetable oil

Makes 18 crêpes

Blend flour, milk, egg, and salt.
Heat lightly oiled 6-in. skillet on
conventional range. Pour 2
tablespoons batter in skillet;
cook until golden brown on
bottom. Turn over. Brown other
side. Repeat with remaining
batter. Use in one of the
following crêpe recipes.

NOTE: Leftover crêpes may
be frozen between 2 layers of
wax paper.

Per Serving:
    Calories: 31
    Sodium: 25 mg.
    Cholesterol: 15 mg.
    Exchanges: ½ bread, ½ fat

◄ Apple Crêpes

8 crêpes, above
¼ cup orange juice
1 teaspoon cornstarch
⅛ teaspoon ground allspice
2 cups unpeeled, chopped
    apples, ¼-in. pieces
2 tablespoons vanilla low fat
    yogurt
⅛ teaspoon orange extract

Serves 8

In 1-qt. casserole combine
orange juice, cornstarch and
allspice. Stir in apples; cover.
Microwave at High 7 to 9
minutes, or until apples soften
and sauce thickens, stirring
once or twice. Place 1
tablespoon mixture on each
crêpe; roll up around filling.

In small bowl combine yogurt
and extract. Top each crêpe
with ¾ teaspoon mixture.

Per Serving:
    Calories: 49
    Sodium: 25 mg.
    Cholesterol: 15 mg.
    Exchanges: ½ fruit, ½ bread,
                     ½ fat

Banana Crêpes ▲

8 crêpes, opposite
1 cup diet cream soda
2 teaspoons cornstarch
½ teaspoon ginger
1 teaspoon cinnamon
3 ripe bananas, cut into ½-in.
   chunks
¼ cup vanilla low fat yogurt
   Dash cinnamon
   Dash nutmeg

Serves 8

In 1-qt. casserole blend soda, cornstarch, ginger and 1 teaspoon cinnamon. Stir in bananas. Microwave at High 3½ to 6½ minutes, or until thickened, stirring 2 or 3 times.

Place 3 tablespoons of banana mixture on each crêpe; roll up around filling.

In small bowl blend yogurt, dash of cinnamon and dash of nutmeg. Top each crêpe with 1½ teaspoons of yogurt mixture.

Per Serving:
   Calories: 91
   Sodium: 29 mg.
   Cholesterol: 15 mg.
   Exchanges: 1½ fruit, ½ bread,
                  ½ fat

Raspberry Cheese ▲ Crêpes

8 crêpes, opposite
1 cup low fat cottage cheese
⅓ cup low sugar red
   raspberry jam
¾ teaspoon vanilla extract
¼ teaspoon cinnamon
⅛ teaspoon nutmeg
2 tablespoons low sugar
   red raspberry jam

Serves 8

In small mixing bowl combine cottage cheese, ⅓ cup jam, vanilla, cinnamon and nutmeg. Microwave at 50% (Medium) 1 to 2½ minutes, or until mixture is heated and jam dissolves, stirring once or twice. Place 1½ tablespoons filling on each crêpe; roll up around filling. Microwave remaining jam at High 45 seconds to 1¼ minutes, or until melted. Drizzle ¾ teaspoon over each crêpe.

Per Serving:
   Calories: 69
   Sodium: 95 mg.
   Cholesterol: 18 mg.
   Exchanges: ½ bread, ½ low fat
                  meat, ½ fat

Mocha Crêpes ▲

8 crêpes, opposite
1 envelope (1 oz.)
   low calorie chocolate
   pudding mix
1 cup skim milk
½ cup water
1½ teaspoons instant coffee
¼ cup plus 8 teaspoons
   prepared low calorie
   whipped topping

Serves 8

In 1-qt. measure blend pudding mix, milk, water and coffee. Microwave at High 3 to 7 minutes, or until bubbly and slightly thickened, stirring every 2 minutes with wire whip. Place plastic wrap directly on pudding to avoid skin formation. Cool to room temperature. Blend in ¼ cup whipped topping.

Place 2 tablespoons pudding mixture on each crêpe; roll up around filling. Top each crêpe with 1½ to 2 teaspoons pudding mixture and 1 teaspoon whipped topping.

Per Serving:
   Calories: 78
   Sodium: 43 mg.
   Cholesterol: 15 mg.
   Exchanges: 1 fruit, ½ bread,
                  ½ fat

Two Layer Mold ▲

2 cans (12 oz. each) diet
  black cherry soda
2 tablespoons unflavored
  gelatin
¾ cup prepared low calorie
  whipped topping
2 cups dark, sweet cherries,
  frozen, defrosted and
  drained

Serves 8

Pour soda into medium mixing
bowl. Sprinkle gelatin over
soda. Microwave at High 2
minutes, or until gelatin
dissolves, stirring once. Chill
to soft set stage.

Add half of gelatin mixture to
whipped topping; whip. Fold in
1 cup of cherries. Set aside.

Combine remaining cherries
with remaining gelatin mixture.
Pour into 4-cup mold. Chill until
soft set. Pour topping mixture
over mixture in mold. Chill until
firm. Unmold and serve.

Per Serving:
  Calories: 47
  Sodium: 18 mg.
  Cholesterol: 0
  Exchanges: ½ fruit, ½ meat

Chocolate Cream Mousse

1 envelope (1 oz.) low
  calorie chocolate
  pudding mix
1½ cups skim milk
  ½ teaspoon Grand Marnier
  ½ teaspoon butter flavoring
  1 egg white
  2 teaspoons fructose
  4 tablespoons prepared low
  calorie whipped topping

Serves 4

In small mixing bowl combine
pudding mix and milk.
Microwave at High 5 to 7
minutes, or until slightly
thickened, stirring 2 or 3 times.
Stir in Grand Marnier and butter
flavoring. Cover top of pudding
with wax paper. Let cool.

In small bowl combine egg
white and fructose. Whip until
egg whites form stiff peaks.
Fold in pudding. Spoon into
serving dishes; chill. Serve with
whipped topping.

Per Serving:
  Calories: 97
  Sodium: 65 mg.
  Cholesterol: 0
  Exchanges: 1 bread, ½ fat

Orange Fruit Bake

2 large bananas, halved
  lengthwise, cut into
  1-in. pieces
2 large oranges, peeled and
  sectioned
¼ cup green grapes, halved
¼ cup orange juice
1 teaspoon rum extract
1 tablespoon water
¼ teaspoon grated orange rind
2 teaspoons brown sugar

Serves 4

Divide fruit evenly into 4 custard
cups. Set aside. Combine
orange juice, rum extract, water
and orange rind in 1-cup
measure. Microwave at High 1
to 1½ minutes, or until boiling.
Pour sauce over fruit in custard
cups; stir to coat fruit. Sprinkle
each fruit cup with ½ teaspoon
brown sugar. Let stand 10
minutes. Cover with wax paper.

Microwave at High 2 to 2½
minutes, or until bananas begin
to soften, rotating once during
cooking. Serve warm.

Per Serving:
  Calories: 123
  Sodium: 2 mg.
  Cholesterol: 0
  Exchanges: 3 fruit

Blueberry Tarts

Crust:
1 tablespoon margarine or
   butter
¼ cup graham cracker crumbs

Filling:
2 tablespoons water
1 tablespoon cornstarch
1 tablespoon fructose
¼ teaspoon cinnamon
1 tablespoon lemon juice
1 pint fresh blueberries

Meringue:
1 egg white
⅛ teaspoon cream of tartar
1 teaspoon fructose
¼ teaspoon cinnamon

Serves 6

Per Serving:
Calories: 96
Sodium: 46 mg.
Cholesterol: 6 mg.
Exchanges: 1 fruit, ½ bread,
             ½ fat

How to Microwave Blueberry Tarts

Melt margarine in small bowl at High 1 to 1½ minutes. Add crumbs and toss. Pat crumb mixture evenly into bottoms of 6 custard cups.

Arrange cups in circle in oven. Microwave at High 1½ minutes, or until set. Set aside. In 1-cup measure combine all filling ingredients except blueberries.

Pour mixture over blueberries in medium bowl; toss to coat. Microwave at High 4 to 5½ minutes, or until thickened, stirring every 1½ minutes. Cool.

Spoon 3 tablespoons of thickened blueberries onto each prepared crust in custard cups. Set aside.

Beat egg white in medium bowl until frothy. Beat in cream of tartar, fructose and cinnamon until stiff peaks form. Mound meringue on top of tarts.

Microwave at High 45 to 60 seconds, or until meringue is set, rotating cups after 30 seconds. Chill before serving.

Raspberry Chiffon

2 cans (12 oz. each) diet
   raspberry soda
3 tablespoons unflavored
   gelatin
¾ cup prepared low calorie
   whipped topping
1 tablespoon graham
   cracker crumbs

Serves 8

In medium bowl combine soda
and gelatin. Microwave at High
3 to 4 minutes, or until gelatin
dissolves, stirring 2 or 3 times.
Chill until soft set. Blend in
topping with hand mixer. Pour
into 9 × 5-in. loaf dish. Top with
crumbs. Chill until set.

Per Serving:
   Calories: 40
   Sodium: 20 mg.
   Cholesterol: 0
   Exchanges: 1 low fat meat

Chocolate Mint Tapioca Pudding

2 pkgs. (¾ oz. each) low
   calorie instant hot
   cocoa mix
1¼ cups water
2 tablespoons quick-cooking
   tapioca
2 teaspoons fructose
¼ teaspoon mint extract
2 eggs, separated
⅛ teaspoon cream of tartar

Serves 6

In medium bowl combine all
ingredients except egg whites
and cream of tartar. Beat with a
wire whip. Microwave at High
3½ to 5½ minutes, or until
boiling, stirring once or twice.
Boil 1 minute. Cool to room
temperature. Set aside.
Beat egg whites with cream of
tartar until soft peaks form. Fold
egg whites into tapioca mixture.
Serve immediately or chill.

Per Serving:
   Calories: 112
   Sodium: 56 mg.
   Cholesterol: 12 mg.
   Exchanges: ½ milk, 1 fruit, ½
                    med. fat meat

Ginger Peach Parfait ▲

1 pkg. (1⅔ oz.) low calorie
   vanilla pudding mix
1½ cups skim milk
1 cup drained, chopped
   peaches
1 cup prepared low calorie
   whipped topping
¼ teaspoon cinnamon
¼ teaspoon ginger
¼ teaspoon nutmeg

Serves 4

In medium bowl blend pudding mix and milk. Microwave at High 4
to 6 minutes, or until slightly thickened, stirring 2 or 3 times during
cooking. Stir in peaches. Cover with plastic wrap. Chill until set.
Blend spices into whipped topping. In each of 4 parfait glasses
layer ¼ cup chilled pudding mix, 3 tablespoons whipped topping,
¼ cup pudding and 1 tablespoon topping.

Per Serving:
   Calories: 163   Cholesterol: 0
   Sodium: 64 mg.   Exchanges: 1 fruit, 1 bread, ½ high fat meat

Baked Pears ▲

2 fresh Bartlett pears
¼ cup orange juice
1 tablespoon raisins
¼ teaspoon grated orange peel
1 teaspoon cornstarch
¼ cup water
    Dash allspice
⅛ teaspoon cinnamon

Serves 4

Cut pears in half lengthwise. Pierce inside of pear halves with fork. Arrange cut side up in 8 × 8-in. baking dish.

In 2-cup measure combine orange juice, raisins, orange peel, cornstarch, water, allspice and cinnamon. Microwave at High 1 to 3 minutes, or until thickened, stirring once or twice. Pour glaze over pear halves. Cover with wax paper.

Microwave at High 4 to 6 minutes, or until tender, rearranging and basting with glaze once during cooking. Let stand 5 minutes. Serve warm with sauce.

Per Serving:
Calories: 53
Sodium: 0
Cholesterol: 0
Exchanges: 1 fruit

Autumn Pudding

1 pkg. (12 oz.) frozen cooked
    squash
1 tablespoon brown sugar
½ teaspoon cinnamon
¼ teaspoon nutmeg
⅛ teaspoon ginger
⅛ teaspoon ground cloves
1 egg, slightly beaten
½ cup buttermilk
2 tablespoons prepared low
    calorie whipped topping
Serves 4

Place squash in 1-qt. casserole. Microwave at High 4 minutes, or until defrosted, stirring to break apart. Stir in sugar and spices. Microwave at High 2 minutes, or until hot, stirring once.

In small bowl combine egg and buttermilk. Add a small amount of hot squash. Stir back into remaining squash. Reduce power to 50% (Medium). Microwave 3½ to 4½ minutes, or until slightly thickened, stirring 2 or 3 times. Place ⅓ cup of the mixture into each custard cup. Chill to set. Chill remaining squash mixture, then combine with whipped topping. Divide evenly between custard cups. Chill.

Per Serving:
Calories: 100
Sodium: 58 mg.
Cholesterol: 72 mg.
Exchanges: 1 bread, ½ med.
                 fat meat

Egg Custard

3 eggs
2 tablespoons fructose
¾ teaspoon vanilla
¼ teaspoon salt, optional
¼ teaspoon nutmeg, divided
½ cup skim milk
¼ cup water

Serves 6

In small bowl beat eggs, fructose, vanilla, salt and ⅛ teaspoon nutmeg until smooth. Set aside.

Combine millk and water in 2-cup measure. Microwave at High 1½ to 2 minutes, or until mixture is hot but not boiling. Stir in egg mixture until smooth. Pour into individual custard cups. Top with remaining nutmeg. Reduce power to 50% (Medium). Microwave 3½ to 4½ minutes, or until soft set, turning and rearranging every 30 seconds. Serve chilled.

Variation:
Low Cholesterol Egg Custard:
Use ¾ cup egg substitute instead of eggs. Microwave at 50% (Medium) 4 to 6 minutes; turn and rearrange every 30 seconds.

Per Serving:
Calories: 57
Sodium: 71 mg.
Cholesterol: 138 mg.
Exchanges: ½ fruit, ½ med. fat
                 meat

Convenience Diet Foods

Going on a diet no longer means that you have to prepare everything from scratch. Many diet convenience foods are available from your supermarket. When you're in a hurry, look for "light" canned soups, egg substitutes, gravy and pudding mixes, and diet TV dinners and frozen entrées.

How to Microwave Diet Pudding Mix (2⅛ oz. box)

Place 1 envelope pudding mix in 1½-qt. casserole or 4-cup measure. Blend in 2 cups skim milk. Stir until pudding dissolves, and is well blended.

Microwave at High 4 to 7 minutes, or until pudding begins to thicken, stirring every 1 to 2 minutes. Cool. Pudding thickens as it stands.

How to Microwave Egg Substitutes (½ cup)

Pour ½ cup (1 carton) defrosted liquid egg substitute into 2-cup measure or bowl.

Microwave at High 1 to 1½ minutes, or until eggs begin to set, stirring after every 30 seconds, pushing cooked portions to center.

Remove eggs from oven while they are still soft and moist. Let stand 1 to 2 minutes. Eggs continue to cook while standing. Stir before serving.

How to Microwave Diet TV Dinners (15 to 16 oz.)

Remove foil from tray. Return tray to box. Microwave at High 5 minutes; rotate ¼ turn after half the time. Remove from box.

Stir vegetables; rearrange or turn over main course, if possible. (If dinner is non-stirrable, let stand 5 minutes.)

Cover tray with wax paper if surface appears dry. Microwave at High 4 to 7 minutes, or until internal temperature is 140°.

How to Microwave Diet Entrées (8 to 13 oz.)

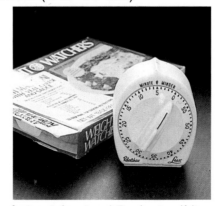

Remove foil from tray. Return tray to box. Microwave at High 5 minutes; rotate ¼ turn after half the time.

Let entrée stand 5 minutes if it is non-stirrable. Remove from box. (If entrée is stirrable, stir after standing time.)

Cover tray with wax paper if surface appears dry. Microwave at High 2 to 10 minutes, or until internal temperature is 140°.

Index